Messages With A Mission

Sermons with Substance

I Cor. 2:1

Wade Burton

Wade Burton

This book is dedicated to my two children. Sharon DePalma, who lives at Surf Side, South Carolina. And to my son, Michael Wade Burton, who left for Heaven on January 11, 2006.

FOREWORD

A salesman stopped overnight in Vermont. He casually walked amid towns-people sitting in chairs on the sidewalk. He would say hello to them, and they would respond with a nod. After several attempts at conversing with them, he asked, "Don't you people have anything to say?" An old timer responded, "We don't speak unless we can improve on the silence."

The sermons in this book are crafted to present some basics in Bible truths and challenges to both reader and hearer. You will discover I have tried to write in a simple, conversational type style. It is hoped by the writer that these sermons will reach the heart and the will of believers who have a desire to grow in spiritual maturity. Extensive Bible exposition has been avoided in order to make the messages easy to read and to be understood.

One of my favorite Bible verses is Matthew 5:7, "Blessed are they which do hunger and thirst after righteousness, for they shall be filled." It is my prayer that the reader who thirsts after God will be satisfied as they share my thoughts in this book.

God bless,

Wade Thompson Burton

I sincerely want to thank my extended daughter, Elaine Lester for typing, editing, proof-reading, and her additional help in preparing this book for publication.

Messages With A Mission

Contents

*"Real praying puts you in contact with God,
and in contract with God."*

THE AWESOME POWER OF PRAYER

Jeremiah 33:3

After 52 years of pastoral ministry I am convinced that no church, nor any Christian, ever grows beyond their prayers of personal repentance and redemptive outreach. <u>Inward cleansing and outward compassion.</u>

In days of the early church, the people would pray ten days, preach ten minutes, and many souls would be saved. Today we pray ten minutes, preach ten days and get ecstatic if anybody is saved!

These routine Sunday Morning prayers won't get it done: "Lord, here we are again. You blessed us last Sunday - bless us again today, and we'll see you again next Sunday."

**Note Little Brother in the following story:

Big Sister and Little Brother were out in the country walking along a road back to their aunt's home. They decided to cut across a pasture to shorten their walk. About half way across, a bull came charging out of the woods. Big Sister made it to a tree and climbed up. The arms of Little Brother were too short to reach a limb. So Big Sister yelled, "Run, Little Brother, run." And Little Brother ran toward the barbed-wire fence. As he got close to the fence, Big Sister yelled, "Slide, Little Brother, slide." Little Brother slid —-into the barbed wire. And there he hung with his backside toward the oncoming bull. Quickly summing up the situation, Big Sister hollered, "Pray, Little Brother, pray." And Little Brother prayed the only prayer he could remember, "I thank Thee for what I am about to receive."

13

Now, let's think about "The Awesome Power of Prayer." And to make you more receptive to the message, I will put us on the same playing field with this confession. All of us need to pray more than we do. Most of the time our problem is not <u>unanswered</u> prayer, but <u>unoffered</u> prayer.

A favorite text that needs to be underscored and kept in your memory is Jeremiah 33:3, "Call unto me and I will answer thee, and show thee great and mighty things which thou knowest not."

I. REAL PRAYING PUTS US IN CONTACT AND CONTRACT WITH ALMIGHTY GOD.

1. The text tells us: "You call" — **Contact!**
                        "I will answer thee." **Contract!**

The result will be happenings beyond our imaginations and expectations.

**I was to preach a revival in Edgefield, South Carolina. The Tuesday before the revival was to begin on Sunday, I awoke with pain running up my back and into my neck. A trip to the doctor on Thursday revealed I had the Shingles. It is a very irritable attack on the nerve system. Riding down the road next Sunday morning I told my wife that I was in trouble. I had undergone sleepless nights. The pain was still acute. Just before I preached, I asked all the deacons to come to the altar and lay hands on me, asking God to give me strength and freedom to preach. I walked back into the pulpit and delivered the message God had put on my heart. I felt no pain. There was not one bit of itching nor discomfort, until I stopped preaching. Each night of the revival, the same thing happened. God seemed to have put a special umbrella of grace over me while I was preaching. I told the congregation I thought I might want to put my bed in the pulpit so I could get some needed rest and sleep. This was an outright miracle. And together, we thanked God and celebrated. God showed the congregation and me a personal "great and mighty thing."

2. We ought to pray because we have **a mighty adversary** - Satan. He can overcome us. He can overwhelm us. He can defeat us. He knows who you are. He knows your address. He knows your strength and he knows your weaknesses. He wants to control you, and if he cannot control you, he will try to cripple and curtail your testimony for the Lord. He was brazen enough to attack our Lord in the wilderness. (See Matt.4:1)

Do you understand the intent and insult of those verses? Satan is your worst enemy, and he is always working to keep you <u>ignorant</u> of the Word of God, <u>indifferent</u> to the will of God, and <u>independent</u> of the work of God.

- — Every tear that falls unbidden from the eyes of broken-hearted men and women,
- — Every heart that is burdened and disappointed,
- — Every dream that is crushed,
- — Every life that is ruined,
- — Every family that is divided is the work of him whom Jesus called, "A liar and a murderer from the beginning." John 8:44.

**Even the Apostle Paul saw himself tempted and weakened by the assault of Satan. And you hear him cry out in Romans 7:24, "O wretched man that I am. Who shall deliver me from the body of death?" And his answer should be your answer and my answer: "I thank God — (it is) through Jesus Christ, our Lord."

3. We ought to pray because we have **an Almighty Ally** in the Lord. The Apostle warns in 1 Peter 5:8, "Be sober, be vigilant - because your adversary, the devil, as a roaring lion, walketh about seeking whom he may desire."

And if you do anything positive in the name of God, He will target you. But our ally says. "I will uphold thee with the right hand of my righteousness. "Isaiah 41:10, "Fear thou not, for I am with thee. Be not dismayed, for I am GOD. I will strengthen thee, yea I will help thee."

The very best thing you can do to overcome that which seems to overcome you is to release it to God. (Not, "You take care of it while I sleep") Rather, you must make a definite commitment to His care in your time of darkness and doubt. Commit it to Him. Entrust it to Him. Expect personal victory from Him. Celebrate! "Let all those that put their trust in Thee rejoice...because Thou defendest them." Psalm 5:11.

Remember this unbreakable promise in Isaiah 43:2, "When thou passest through the waters, I will be with thee; and through the rivers, they shall not overflow thee. When thou walkest through the fire, thou shalt not be burned, neither shall the flame kindle upon thee." Amen and amen!!!

4. We should pray because prayer is the most potent power source within our reach.

**I am amazed at the power of nature around us. Scientists tell us there is in every drop of water in every ocean enough energy to generate two thunderstorms. One of the most powerful forces in nature is radium. It is a million times more powerful than dynamite. In days before diesel engines, when it took 12,000 tons of coal to drive a steamship 6,000 miles at fifteen knots, the same result can be produced with 22 ounces of radium. Why do I tell you that? Not to try to give you a lesson in physics; rather, to point you to the One Who designed it, and gave men the sense to use it. And it is Almighty God who invites you to partake in His power, His provisions and protection.

I believe Christians have within their reach, resources to make a better world, and certainly to make a better you.

**Dr. Courtland Rice, a renowned scientist has said, "The prayer of faith is mightier than any dynamite, because it has the almightiness of God linked to it."

II. PRAYER REACHES BEHIND CLOSED DOORS

1. There is no secret nor sinful heart, you cannot penetrate with prayer. Do you know a neighbor who is unchurched? Talk with God about them first. Then find an opportunity to talk with them about God. Pray for them before you talk with them. Ask the Holy Spirit to prepare them for your intervention on their behalf. I'll have to admit, I have done the above. And when I was moved by God's Spirit to know the time was ripe, I put my prayers into action with a personal visit with that person. And I was overwhelmed because of their readiness to talk about their spiritual lostness and their readiness to receive God's salvation.

**I recall trying to reach a man whose three daughters belonged to our church. I prayed for him more than I visited him. Then one day one of his neighbors died. And I preached his funeral. And this was the only time in fifty-four years of ministry that I preached a fully evangelistic funeral sermon. At the graveside, this man for whom I had prayed, told me, "I'll see you in church Sunday." And next Sunday morning this man, who was in his sixties, came down the aisle and publicly accepted Jesus Christ as his personal Saviour. I prayed and the Holy Spirit worked. Prayer can reach behind closed doors and closed hearts.

2. Prayer can also reach beyond closed borders in foreign countries. How many times have you and I visited Russia through prayer? How many times have you gone beyond closed doors in countries of Africa, in prayer? How many times have we visited needy countries all over the world through intercessory prayer?

**William Carey lived in England. Born in 1793 and died in 1833. He was a cobbler by trade. In his shop he had a map of the world. And he prayed for lost people in foreign countries everyday, that someone would go to reach them, and minister to them for Jesus. At a church meeting Carey asked the preachers what was being done to reach the heathen. He was told, "Young man, sit down! When God pleases to convert the heathen world, He will do it without your help or mine." This did not discourage this man who could read the Bible in six different languages. He would select a heathen nation and pray for the unreached souls who lived there. When there was further talk about reaching the heathen, someone asked, "Who will go? "And Carey responded, "I will go." His wife and four children accompanied him on this long journey. He had to work to support his family. It took seven years of labor and prayers for him to reach his first convert. Carey had visited the country in prayer before he visited it in person. The doors opened to him because he had been there many times before in prayers of compassion and and conviction.

It is the same old wonderful story of our mission efforts through our mission board. People pray for doors to open. And now we are entrenched and ministering to people in more than 200 countries around the world. It is reported we are winning more than one thousand souls to Jesus each day. PRAISE THE LORD!!! Doors for witnessing have been opened behind Iron and Bamboo curtains.

Carey had said, "Attempt great things for God. Expect great things from God." Priorities are most important in your witness, or your non-witness for Christ. Carey had a small sign in his shop: **"God first. Family second. Shoes third."** What is first in your life? This is the reason for the results you get, or results you fail to get.

III. PRAYER ACTIVATES FEEBLE FAITH

1. "But I just don't feel like praying," the more reason for you to pray. You don't feel much because you have not expected much. Perhaps you have not expected much because you have not prayed much.

2. When you truly reach up and touch God in prayer, you might get a shock. But hold on, and you will get a spiritual charge! "The prayers of the righteous availeth much." James 5:16

**When Dwight David Eisenhower was inaugurated as President of the United States in January, 1953, he surprised the nation by offering up a personal prayer to God.

—He knew his task was extraordinarily large.
—He knew he needed Divine enabling.
—He believed the Enabler was One who responded to sincere praying.

He later explained, "To the best of my knowledge, the men of courage I have known have been men of faith. I've never seen any of them who weren't."

** A child knelt by her bedside and prayed: "Dear God, if You're up there, and you hear my prayer, could you please just touch me?" She felt a light touch on her shoulder. Excitedly she prayed: "Thank You God for touching me." As she rises from her knees, she saw her older sister standing behind her. She asks, "Did you touch me?" "Yes I did," said sister. "Why did you do it?" "Because," said sister, "God told me to do it." WELL? Figure that one out for yourself.

I know I need to touch you on God's behalf, to tell you to pray more, and to expect more. To allow His Kingdom to become so real in your own life, that you may be guided to make the Kingdom real for your associates, family and friends.

3. Prayer can become needed purging that gets out a lot of garbage within, in order to allow purity to enter. Purity leads to empowerment.

IV. PRAYER YIELDS SURPRISING SPIRITUAL HARVESTS

1. I remember reading about a missionary family in a foreign country. The children were praying and asking God to do certain things for them. One child loved Rice Crispies. But none was available in that country. This boy prayed and asked God to send him some of this special cereal. A week or two later a large container arrived from the States. The lad said, "I bet God has sent me some Rice Crispies." In the box were a lot of personal items for members of the family. And in that care package was a box of cereal. Corn Flakes! The boy

looked and was disappointed. He was told, "At least God sent you some cereal." That day when he opened the cornflake box, it was filled with Rice Crispies! Again, <u>figure that one out</u>.

2. I've shared this story many times. When I lived at Coronaca and served in my first church, there was a family who lived below us. The wife attended church when her health permitted. Their two daughters united with us and were baptized. Their daddy was an alcoholic, and he refused to come to church. After a while we planned a revival for Coronaca Baptist. One week before the revival, Jerry was headed home from work. I was in my front yard.

When I saw Jerry turning the corner, I quickly prayed, "Lord, let me talk to Jerry." His car stalled. I went down to the car and asked, "Jerry, what's your trouble?" He used an expletive and said, "This car just stopped running."

I talked about his family, and invited him to church. He was very negative. That same week, I was in the yard about 5:30 P.M. Jerry turned the corner to go home. "Lord, will you do it again?" The car stopped. A week later we started the revival. On Tuesday night Jerry showed up. At the invitation he rushed out of the church. On Wednesday, the same thing happened. On Thursday, instead of going out the door, he came to the altar. I asked him "What's happening, Jerry?" He responded, "I don't know. I'm all mixed up and I need some help." I told him, "Jerry, this is the Lord dealing with your heart. He wants you to get saved. Are you ready to let Him forgive you and enter your heart and life?" "YES," was his answer. Jerry was the direct result of answered prayer. PRAISE THE LORD!!! Jerry is residing with Jesus in Heaven today.

CONCLUSION

Beloved, are you now aware of the power God makes available to you through your praying? Are you ready to let that power become real in your walk with God, and your talk for God?

If you came through those doors today with emptiness and hope-lessness, pray, in Jesus name, and God will relieve you of your guilt and sin. He will release you to be empowered to win your family, your neighbors and your co-workers to Him. WILL YOU DO IT? Right now!

Amen!

"You cannot possess the peace that Christ has brought until you have asked for His pardon."

ONCE UPON A TIME

Genesis 1:1-2

Once upon a time there was no "Once upon a time" on this earth. (Read Genesis 1:1-2) — and the story grows from there.

1. God created:
    He created the light, vs.3
    He created the water, and then He created the land.
    He created grass, and trees.
    He created the seasons, the stars and the moon.
    He created the creatures of the sea and birds of the air.
    On the sixth day He created land animals.
    Last of all, He created man to be like unto Himself.

2. Man was given the right to choose for himself. And the first man, Adam, and his wife Eve, chose what the Lord told them not to choose. They violated the holy covenant, allowing sin to come into the world to rule and to ruin the family of man.

3. This breach caused a vast chasm between them and the Person and presence of the Lord. Their sin separated them from God and His holiness.

4. The Lord devised a plan to bring man back into fellowship with Him. This plan was called Redemption. The basic plan of redemption was tied into man's discipline of keeping God's Law, until the day Jesus Christ would come to earth to secure a "once for all" salvation for believers. Animal sacrifice was established as forerunners for the time when the God's special Lamb would die vicariously on Calvary.

5. The story unfolds with the archangel Gabriel being appointed to come down to earth to tell Mary she had been selected to be the mother of the Christ Child. Mary is startled to see someone in her room. She asks, "Who are you?" "I'm Gabriel, and I have come from God to tell you He has elected you to become the mother of the Christ-Child." "Wait a minute," said Mary, "I'm not even wedded; yet, I am engaged, but I have not yielded myself to any man." Gabriel understood her anxiety. "The Holy Spirit of God is going to come upon you. You will become the mother to give birth to God's promised Messiah." "Let God's will be done," said Mary.

6. And Christ's coming to earth is the basic story of Christmas.

7. And Christmas reminds us that Christ, indeed, came down to this world in the form of a precious Baby. This Jesus, this Christ of God, came among us to redeem us.

I. HE CAME TO OFFER PARDON FOR OUR SINS AND TO GIVE PEACE TO OUR SOULS.

1. Pardon is the offer of forgiveness to the guilty ones. Ezra, the prophet, made a confession that ought to be our confession if we are to connect with God, "O my God, I am ashamed and blush to lift up my face to Thee; for our iniquities are increased over our head, and our trespass is grown up unto the heavens." Ezra 9:6. If you don't understand what Ezra is saying in the KJV, listen to this paraphrase from the Living Bible, Ezra (9:5-6) "I stood before the Lord in great embarrassment; then I fell to my knees and lifted my hands to the Lord, and cried out, 'Oh my God, I am ashamed; I blush to lift up my face to You. (WHY?) Because our sins are piled higher than our heads, and our guilt is as boundless as the heavens.'"

The person who said that is somebody who is under the heavy burden of a guilty conscience. That is somebody who needs to get the attention of a forgiving God. That is somebody under the conviction that some changes are needed in his life. Is there anybody here who feels this need within your heart today? If so, I have good news for you. God is dealing with your life. He is ready to bring remedy to your spiritual tragedy. He is ready to make the Christ of Christmas real to you.

**The psalmist expressed it this way in Ps. 40:12. For "my sins, too many to count, have all caught up with me, and I am ashamed to look up (to Thee). My heart quails within me." Quails" means, "All shook up." His guilt over his failures is tearing him apart. And I want to tell you there is no antidote for this guilt that can be found in a bottle, whether by prescription or in a bottle of booze. Guilt within the soul cannot be erased by counseling, nor can it be removed by the comforting of a friend. There is only One Person who can reach back into your yesterdays and erase those uneraseable sins, the awesome blight of human gone-wrongness.

But let me hasten to tell you that guilt is good. It means your conscience is working. It means God has not given up on you. It means the Holy Spirit can now direct you to ask the Lord for your own pardon, trusting Him to do His perfect cleansing. And I pray you will be willing to ask for it, as though your life is depending on it. It is certain that your eternal soul depends upon it. Never play around with guilt. Never put off confessing your guilt when the Holy Spirit brings it to your attention. For this is the time when God's pardon is being offered to you.

2. Now I want to ask you, do you personally have God's pardon? Have you taken time to ask for it? Let me advise you, you cannot possess the peace that Christ has brought, until you have asked for His pardon. And when you ask for it in sincerity, God has already committed Himself to respond with His forgiveness to you; and after forgiveness, comes His peace. He told Israel, and He tells us in Jer.31:34,"I will forgive their iniquity, and I will remember their sin no more." What an offer! What a contract!

"(When) we confess our sins, He is faithful and just to forgive us our sins, and to cleanse us from all unrighteousness." John 1:9. You will be at peace with him. He has proffered it and He has provided it. It is yours for the asking. That gift God brings to you today. Listen, Jesus was chastised and crucified to give us His unique peace. Peace with God and personal peace within our own hearts.

**The host of Heaven told the shepherds the night of His birth: "Glory to God in the highest, and on earth, peace and goodwill toward men." Luke 1:79b tells us Jesus came "to guide our feet into the way of peace."

> Find Jesus, He will give you His pardon.
> Follow Jesus, He will lead you to His peace.

II. BUT THERE IS MORE! BEYOND HIS PARDON AND PEACE IS HIS PROMISE AND PROVISION FOR AN ETERNAL HOME WITH HIM IN GLORY.

1. Jesus came to earth to offer every man and woman God's pardon and peace. And now He has gone back to Heaven to prepare a special place for every person who trusts Him to do it for them. "For we know that, if our earthly house (body) were dissolved, we have a building of God, a house not made with hands, eternal in the heavens."2 Cor.5:1. I may not live to see the earthly Jerusalem, but I want to tell you loud and clear, I plan to see the New Jerusalem. Our Dear Lord has promised it. John tells about it in Rev.21:2, "I saw the Holy City, new Jerusalem, coming down from God out of Heaven, prepared as a bride adorned for her husband." I will see it, and I will enjoy it forever, because I have trusted God's Christ to save me a place among that great throng of believers in Glory.

** I once saw the President of the United States, Lyndon Banes Johnson. But I had no urge to praise him, nor bow before him. However I want to tell you something, this Baptist is going to be up there on that great day raising my arms in honor to Him. To the One who came to this earth and died to give me pardon and peace.

2. Christmas is a time of wonder. It reminds us that God has come among us as Jesus, the all-sufficient Christ. And all glory to God, He has invited us to come to Heaven and share this eternal home with Him forever.

"On Jordan's stormy banks I stand, and cast a wishful eye,
To Canaan's fair an happy land, where my possessions lie"

Jesus said it, "Lay not up for yourselves treasures upon earth, where moth and rust doth corrupt, and where thieves break through and steal. But lay up for yourselves treasures in Heaven." Matt.6:19-20. Some of you have done that, and you are doing it today, because you did it yesterday, and you will do it tomorrow. You know where real investments are that pay the greatest dividends of all.

Dear saints of God, you may not understand the trials you have suffered, or you are presently suffering. But God knows, and He will see you through every storm and every dark valley. One day He will stoop down and wipe away those precious tears, and He will put an everlasting smile on your face.

"Trials dark on every hand, and we cannot understand,
All the ways that God would lead us to that blessed
Promised Land;
But He'll guide us with His eye, and we'll follow till we die,
We will understand it better, by and by.

"Temptations, hidden snares, often take us unawares,
And our hearts are made to bleed for some thoughtless
word or deed,
And we wonder why the test, when we try to do our best,
But we'll understand it better by and by.

THE CHORUS

"By and by, when the morning comes,
When the saints of God are gathered home,

27

We will tell the story, how we've overcome,
We will understand it better by and by."
—Charles A. Tindley

And beloved, I can hardly wait for that day. It is for that day that Jesus came to make it possible for you and me to enter His heavenly home, ever to be with Him and all the saints in Glory.

And if you have never come to Him Who came to you, then come today.

Receive His pardon and peace. Get ready to go Home with Him. Amen!

"God has no Plan B."

CHILDREN OF THE KINGDOM

Daniel 2:44-45

My Father is rich in houses and lands, He holdeth the wealth
of the world in His hand. Of rubies and diamonds, of silver and
gold - His coffers are full, He has riches untold.
A tent or a cottage, why should I care? He's building a palace
for me over there. Tho' exiled from home, yet still I may sing,
All glory to God, I'm a child of the King. —Hattie Buell

1. It excites me to know that I am a child in the Kingdom of God. It
should excite you to know you are a child in the Father's kingdom.
This relationship has come by Divine adoption. I've been adopted
into God's family. Celebrate with me.

> If you have asked Christ to forgive you of your sins,
> If you have asked Jesus to come into your heart,
> If you have this relationship validated by living for Him,
> Walking with Him, leaning on Him, fellowshipping with Him.
> Then, I celebrate with you!

2. When we come together in God's House, it is time for celebration,
Not condemnation!

This silent, sickening, frowning, criticizing, backbiting, non-smiling
kind of faithlessness by an unsaved church member is an abomina-
tion to the King and His Kingdom.

> —If you have the kind of faith that is always creating hostility
>   among the brethren, stop it now!
> —If you come to church to see what Jane Doe is wearing, get
>   your eyes off Jane onto Jesus.

29

—If you come to church expecting nothing, stop it and start to believe Jesus is here to challenge and charge some of us, and those unwilling to be charged up, are candidates to be changed.

3. Come on. Get with it. If you are a child of the King, you've got better blood running through your veins than sinking to the standards of a Christless world.

—You need to change your motives if you are a gossip. Tell your King today that you are ready to stop gossiping about your brother and sister in Christ, and you're ready to start gossiping the Gospel.
—Start acting like a child of the King. You are in His Kingdom, not to localize your agenda of trifles, but to celebrate with your brothers and sisters the great Kingdom of God and His Kingdom of grace. And every Christian should have thought, or said "AMEN!"

4. We are told in God's Word: "The Kingdom of Heaven is at hand." Matthew 4:17. We are told in Matthew 6:33 to, "Seek ye first the Kingdom of God, and His righteousness." To do this you have to prioritize your present aims and goals. If your main goal is financial success, or sports, or even health, it is probable you will not find the Kingdom in these pursuits. Many people will not make it to Heaven because they spent most of their time giving first-rate loyalties to second-rate causes. Jesus said, "Seek ye first the Kingdom of God and His righteousness..." And what comes next? "All these (other needful) things shall be added unto you." In pursuing the Kingdom of God, you must move everything aside in order to get it. And when you do that, when you realize the Kingdom is the real reason for your existence, you will be willing to lay aside every thing, and anything that blinds your eyes to this Pearl of Great Price.

Now let me turn to a passage of Scripture and show you how you and other people can be in danger of chipping away at the foundation of God here on earth. (See Matthew 12:22-32)

Please get this whole picture? We have a victim with a demon inside. The man is blind and speechless. He is possessed by a damnable spirit. Overmastered by evil.

The critical Pharisees were Bitter! Biting! Negative. Unbowed. Unbending. They accused this unfortunate man of getting what he deserved. Jesus was there to minister, to heal, to recover health, to reconcile a family, to bring wholeness to this unfortunate creature. That's Who Jesus is. He was there, and He is here today to restore wholeness to some of you who have lost it.

But the criticizing Pharisees were there also. They stood by casting suspect on what Jesus was doing to help a fallen human being. They tried to chip away parts of the Kingdom that Jesus was working to enlarge.

Some people spend all their lives building fences, to keep certain people out of their environment. While others in the know, they build bridges for people to come and share their lives, their faith, their dreams, and their destiny. Believers must be very careful, because you can become like the Pharisees. Jealous, Suspicious, Critical. Attempting to build your self up while trying to tear other people down. And all the while you do this, you can be hindering the work of God. Chipping away at His Kingdom. Caution, there is real spiritual danger here. Don't close your heart to the blessings God wants to give to you daily. If you have a fist folded against a brother, you cannot receive anything eternal from the Father.

I. TODAY I INVITE YOU TO HELP ME TO Find and DEFINE THE KINGDOM OF GOD (Read Daniel 2:44-45)

1. What is the Kingdom of God on earth? The Kingdom of God is the firm establishment of God's rule and reign among the kingdom of men.

2. It is the habitation of God on earth. We are told in Matthew 6:33 to "Seek ye first the Kingdom of God and His righteousness. "That

should become our highest priority, our chief aim, to seek until we find what God has provided for us to have:

His purpose, His provision, His power, His Person in Jesus Christ.

3. Do you see it? When we enter into the Kingdom of God through Christ, then Christ brings the Kingdom into our hearts. The Kingdom is all around us, and it is within the hearts of believers. Luke 17:20-2, "The Kingdom of God cometh not with observation." You won't seek it, and find it, and then say "There it is." If you could see it three-dimensionally, you would think it has limits to its boundaries. Your narrow vision would limit it within the confines of this world.

No, the Kingdom of God is a power, a force for good that is not centralized in Washington, D.C., Paris, France, nor even the Vatican. It is found in the hearts and lives of children who are in the Kingdom. Jesus says to believers, "The Kingdom of God is within you." Luke 17:21.

4. The Kingdom defined is **"Basileia,"** God's property. (His children) Basileia = Royalty. Exclusively belonging unto the Lord God. A realm where He is Ruler and King.

Who are the Kingdom residents? SAINTS of God! **"Hageeos"** The pure ones, the blameless ones, the consecrated ones. Colossians 1:2 speaks to believers, "To the saints and faithful brethren at Colosse." It would be correct for me to address you the same way: "To you, the saints at _____ _____.

LISTEN: You who have sought Jesus Christ as Saviour, and found Him, you are saints, not because you have lived, or are presently living perfect lives. You can't become a saint by working 40 years among India's poorest people in India. Nor by climbing a treacherous mountain to Mecca, nor by traveling to another country and kissing a holy person's ring.

You become a saint by your submission to God's commission. "Here I am Father, a sinner filled with pride and selfishness, filled with the flesh and unconquered desires, pettiness within and pollutions without. Lord, I ask You to forgive my failures and sins of the past. There is no eraser big enough for me to blot out my own sins. I ask You to cleanse me of moral and mental filth that lies couched in the corners of my soul, just waiting to break out is some shameful way to hurt me and to harm others. I ask you to enter my heart, to re-program me into the likeness of Your dear Son, the Lord Jesus Christ, Whom I now receive as my personal Redeemer, Saviour and Lord." And God looks at you as He listens to you. He loves you, and I hope you will hear Him say to your soul, "It is done!" You have met my requirement, and now I meet your greatest need. You are forgiven. You are cleansed. You are made whole. You are adopted. You are my child! And from now on, you are to me and to family, and to the world, a SAINT in My household. That is rejoicing time! That is shouting time! That is Amen time!

And apart from that holy personal encounter with the Lord, you cannot be in the Kingdom. John 3:5, "Verily, verily, I say unto you, except a man be born of water, and of the Spirit, he cannot enter into the Kingdom of God." GOD HAS NO PLAN "B."

Dear saints, it is this Divine enactment and enabling that places you inside the Kingdom, and places the Kingdom inside of you. You become righteous and acceptable to God through the atoning blood of Jesus Christ. You are counted righteous through His righteousness. "Abraham believed God, and it was counted unto him for righteousness." Romans 4:3.

Abraham believed = Abraham trusted God to take care of him. To lead him where he had never gone before. And Abraham got to his final destiny, HOW?.............By trusting God to get him there.

Did Abraham have his own roadmap to Canaan land? No. Did Abraham make his own traveling arrangement from earth to Heaven? No. It was His trusting the Lord to take care of that for him. And Abraham is listed among the saints in Hebrews 11:8, "By faith Abraham, when he was called to go out into a place which he should after receive for an inheritance, obeyed. He went out not knowing whither he went." He went out following God. He went on following God. He went UP, following God!

LISTEN, Today you are what you are and where you are by the choices you have made at critical times in your spiritual journey. And these choices will determine your future destiny. If you're comfortable where you are, and you're satisfied with your future expectation of your destiny, then you are either: (a) A Christian resolved to go with God all the way to where He leads you, or (b) You are so confused in your value system that you believe all there is to this life is three-score years and ten. Get all the gusto you can while you can.

If you believe that, you have a world of timelessness to regret your eternal mistakes and blunder. (??) Am I a fool to believe I came into the world through God's power? To believe I will leave this world in God's timing and through God's provision?

If I believe this, and in the end it just isn't true, I will have lost nothing. However, if you disbelieve this and find in eternity you were wrong, you will have lost it all.

Jesus, the One Who came from eternity, and provided a doorway for us to abide with Him in that eternity asked, "What is a man profited if he gains the whole world, and loses his own soul?" The young ruler was very rich, and he made his decision to rely on his riches. He was a man who tithed his income, and still missed Heaven. Will you be so unwise to hold your rusting trinkets to your breast and let them lead you to a final destiny of doom?

LISTEN: <u>GOD'S GREATEST PLEASURE IS TO BE BELIEVED</u>. "Believe on the Lord Jesus Christ, and thou shalt be saved." You don't have to understand all about atonement, justification and adoption. You simply have to believe God has provided it for you through His only begotten Son, Jesus Christ, Saviour and Redeemer.

GOD'S GREATEST PAIN IS TO BE DOUBTED.

To doubt He loves you,
To doubt His Son's sacrifice for you.
To doubt He has Heaven waiting for you.

Your greatest privilege is to trust God. Your greatest peril is to turn your back upon that trust.

II. WE HAVE DISCUSSED THE KINGDOM OF OUR GOD, NOW, WE CLOSE WITH SOME VERY IMPORTANT PERSONAL QUESTIONS

Question No. 1: Where are you most comfortable?

a. Following after the crowd that follows not after Christ? You know where you were last week. Some of you know you would be ashamed for the church to know.

Remember the man who accidentally went into a convention hall where hundreds of preachers were meeting? Later this guy told a friend, **"I felt like a lion in a den of Daniels." Yes, if the place of compromise is your comfort zone, then you need to question your relationship with the King and His Kingdom.

b. Or, Do you find yourself most comfortable with God's people doing God's work? A place where you feel genuine love, and you give back that kind of love. And when we stand and greet one another, the real motive is oneness, acceptance, sameness and forgiveness. The ground is level at the foot of the Cross. All are welcome. All should feel at home.

And for those of you who say, "Well I am not completely comfortable when I am in church, and I am not completely comfortable with worldlings outside the church." I've got news for you. You might think you're standing on neutral ground. But you're not! You might think you're good enough to make it within one foot of Heaven, but let me tell you, in your own righteousness and good deeds, you can get so far up the ladder, but you'll never make it through the gates to Glory.

Question No. 2 What motivates you within to make you what you are?

a. Could it be selfishness? This gives a lot of people a lot of trouble. Exclusiveness? Before Christ took over my life. My world was very exclusive. You didn't get into my world without my permission. My desire to have you inside my world was for you to feed my pride, my ego. You had to agree with my bias. You had to be a "Yes" man to my reasoning. If you didn't do all this, you were welcome to stay out of my fence. Out of my life.

b. But you know, there are a lot of people who were once like me. But now they are changed in character and soul because Jesus came into their heart. He brought with Him a lot of love. And that love now dominates our lives. We now make decisions to be involved in the things that God is involved with.

Our selfishness has been transformed into service for Christ, and service to others in the name of the Lord.

My eyes have become His eyes to see needs all about me.
My ears have become His ears to hear the heart cries of hopeless souls.
My hands have become His hands to reach out to others.
My heart has become His heart to love what He loves.

"We know that we have passed from death unto life, because we love the brethren." I John 3:14. We know we have entered the Kingdom of God because our loves have changed, our wants have changed, our goals have changed, our destinies have changed. We are Kingdom people!

Question No. 3 And please don't fail to hear this last one. If you were to die within the next two minutes, would you go to Heaven, or would you go down to eternal doom? If you don't know where you would go, I want to tell you in love that you probably will not go up! If you do know where you would go, that you would go to Heaven, then I ask you, at this moment, to bow your heads and pray for the unsure, that they will know for sure that they would go to be with God.

Prayer:

Dear Father of the Kingdom, Your children within the Kingdom now praise You for Your matchless gift of adoption into your family. But Lord, the compassion You gave to us is now causing us to pray for those present who are not in Your Kingdom. Holy Spirit of God, we ask for You to come and plead one more time with the unsaved to get saved today. Right now! WE know the gate to the seat of mercy is open. We know that Your voice is calling. Father, help the helpless to know You are reaching out to them at this moment. And Lord, give them the grace to walk by faith into Your Kingdom right now. In Jesus' Name.

OH, WHO WILL COME AND GO WITH ME? I AM BOUND FOR THE PROMISED LAND. Amen and amen!

"Man suffers when he believes the devil's lies and doubts God's Truth."

GOD SAYS IT, THAT SETTLES IT

2 Timothy 3:13-17

1. Some years ago the SBC held its annual meeting in Houston, Texas. My wife and I traveled there with Larry and Marcel Southerland. Larry and Marcel spent 9 years in Japan as SBC missionaries. On our way home, early one morning we stopped outside New Orleans for breakfast. While waiting to be served, I noticed a man at the bar kept looking and smiling at us. (Back then you could smile at strangers without expecting unusual surprises.) He nodded at us and we nodded back. He then walked over to our table and introduced himself. "Hello, I am _____ _____. I attend Mid City Baptist Church. Are y'all Christians?" And before we had a second cup of coffee he told us about Paul Driscoll coming into this community and starting the church by knocking on doors. And how it grew into a huge suburban church with a school system serving hundreds of students through the twelfth grade. "We have a banner stretched across the church auditorium and here's what is says: **'GOD SAYS IT. YOU BELIEVE IT. THAT SETTLES IT.'**

Would you folks like to go and see our church?" We said "No."
> #1 - We hadn't had our breakfast.
> #2 - We didn't feel too cooperative at that time of morning.
> #3 - We really were in a hurry to get home.

2. But I want to tell you that I learned something from that brother:

a. Enthusiastic Christian love will find an outlet for witness.
b. Any place and any time is the right place and time to tell anybody about our Lord.
c. We ought to love our Saviour and His church enough to lovingly invite unchurched people to attend with us.

d. This man was one of the causative factors that Mid City Baptist Church was filled with people every Sunday morning and evening.

3. When I returned home I told my brother Lee about Mid City Baptist and the banner across the front of the church. He immediately responded, "The banner should have read: **GOD SAYS IT. THAT SETTLES IT, WHETHER YOU BELIEVE IT OR NOT.**" I agreed with him.

4. There has always been a battle over God's Word by scholars and non-scholars. The argument was begun by Satan when he asked Eve in Gen.3:1, Yea, hath God said?" Implying to Eve, "God might have said it, but it may not be all true." And since that day, mankind has suffered when believing the devil's lie and doubting God's truth.

Turn in your Bibles and let us read together 2 Tim. 3:16-17. Now let us talk about:

I. THE AUTHORITY OF SCRIPTURE

1. I ask you, where is the church's primary authority for faith and practice? Some would say <u>societal needs</u>. Others say it should be based upon <u>human reasoning</u>; thus opening the door to Universalism, Free Thinking, New Ageism and Dogoodism. There is a group who believe our authority in the church should be directed by Ecclesiastical Dogma - truth interpreted by a church hierarchy. How about special revelation offered by Joseph Smith, Charles Russell, even Buddha?

2. But the Baptists I know believe in Divine Truth revealed in the holy Word of God. We might not understand every jot and tittle, but we accept the parts we don't understand.

** Billy Graham once wrote: "When I began to preach I had some doubts about this Book (Bible). One day in 1949 I opened the Bible and I said, 'Oh God, I don't understand everything in this Book. But from this day on I am going to accept this Book by faith as the authority for my life and ministry." And he later testified, "My ministry changed overnight."

3. In our text in 2 Tim. 3:16-17 the Apostle Paul is declaring the trust-worthi-ness of Scripture and he affirms its place as the final authority for faith, salvation, and for preaching. The King James Version under-scores: "All Scripture is given by inspiration of God."

Now that sounds good and authentic enough for me. But some readers see this as a loop hole to cast forth a faith by their own inter-pretation. For instance, "God inspired Paul to write about Him. That means Paul's writings can be questioned, because Paul could have misunderstood, or perhaps misstated what he thought was inspira-tion from God." There have been all kind of questions by people unwilling to face the truth. "I was inspired to write that poem." Really? By whom? "I was inspired to paint that picture." Inspired of God? Perhaps. Perhaps not.

4. But Paul leaves no open door for lower nor higher criticism, when he states it in Greek in 2 Tim. 3:16 a, "All Scripture is God-breathed." I like that. For it says to me that every word God gave to inspired writers was directed and selected by Him. And it becomes the grounds for all truth and authority. If you failed to catch it, I am an inerrantist in my theology, and so should you be if you want to be empowered to share the Word. Now that position does not mean that I never make errors. It means God gave it in such a way that it, the Bible, is never in error. While God did use the style and personality of the human writer, every word in the original autographs was the product of a Divine fiat. The Bible is God's authentic Word to man, free of error in the original presentation to inspired writers and completely reliable for theology, history, doctrine, science and morals.

AUTOGRAPH is the original manuscript (And there is not a single one that has been found today) Manuscripts are copies of copies. When the scribes copied an autograph, sometimes they would add their own ideas with a comment inserted on the margin. For instance, look at Mark 16:18 "They shall take up serpents." Why don't we go out and capture some of these six-foot rattlesnakes and let our deacons prove their faith by playing with them? BE CAREFUL HERE: The best scholars say the earlier manuscripts do not include this word about taking up snakes. Scholars tell us It was added by a scribe (a copier).

Here is how it might have happened: KJV -1611, Mark 16:18 "They shall take up serpents." An earlier scribe in 1511 could have written: "God can heal a believer who picks up a snake and is bitten." A scribe in 1411: "God can heal a believer even if he is bitten by a snake that is poisonous." Another in 1311: "God can heal all afflictions, even the poisonous sting of a serpent." In 1211: God will protect you from anything that might harm you." Reverse the time sequence above and you can see how this might have happened: When I say the Bible is inerrant, I am speaking of God, and not man's translation or mistranslation.

5. Why is Biblical inerrancy so important? Does it really matter?

a. Yes! Absolutely! If I am going to walk across a deep abyss, I need to know the bridge I am standing on is completely trustworthy. I don't want a map that leads me one foot short of Heaven. I want one that will lead me safely all the way to my eternal home.

An inerrant Word becomes the foundation upon which I stand in belief and behavior. What we believe becomes the guiding authority that influences every decision we make and every step we take. Our whole value system is based upon what we believe, and it governs how we live.

b. How do people form beliefs that determine their behavior? Some people follow cultural patterns. They are shaped by happenings around them. "Monkey see, monkey do." And this is why some people live by standards fashioned by movies, magazines, neighbors and co-workers.

42

Others base their beliefs and behavior on <u>feeling,</u> (Hedonism). "If it feels good, do it." This attitude governs some people within the church and most people not in church. Too many fashion their belief and behavior on <u>church teachings,</u> or cult polity. Whatever the authorities or cult leaders say, those teachings become the guidelines for their conduct. The only trouble with this, what if you have a leader like Jim Jones? There are some "churches" that condemn what others condone. But the Christian inerrantist bases his belief and governs his behavior on Biblical revelation.

**Josh McDowell is a special minister to youth and college students. He says there are three questions that come up in every university campus he visits: Who am I? Why am I here? Where am I headed? The Bible alone gives clear, authoritative answers to these questions. Thus, one reason Biblical inerrancy is so important is that it becomes the foundation for Christian belief and behavior.

It is also the basis for persuasive, anointed teaching and preaching. Some of you should be grateful you have never had to sit under uninspired preaching by preachers uncertain about the Word of God.

**In my years as a preacher, I have bumped into so many congregants who are anemic in the Bible, and so hungry for the Word of God. I have been told by some church members, "We're not being fed." Meaning their pastor did not preach the Word fully, and in an inspiring way. I have tried to be honest and tell them: (1) Pray hard for your pastor to be enlightened. Or, (2) Go to another church where you can be fed by a pastor who preaches the whole counsel of God. And you will find encouragement by a people who believe, obey, teach and share the full Word of God.

**Years ago I had an older pastor tell me: "I am amazed at your pulpit power and sincerity. I told him, "It is the Word, not me. The power is in the Word. I trust the Holy Spirit completely to confirm the Word to listeners. And I preach it without any apology." And most preachers I know who are worth listening to, believe the same thing. Anointed preaching and teaching comes from the authority of God's Word.

c. The unerring Bible points, appoints and positions Christians to do the work of God in the world. True Christians become concerned about God's concern for a lost and straying world. I believe every Christian is to be God's ambassador and missionary at home and abroad. Christians who know they are reading an inerrant Bible will take seriously God's mandate of personal witnessing. They are the ones who now are aggressively witnessing and winning the lost to come to Jesus Christ. Today the U.S.A has 457,000 ordained ministers to take care of over 250 million people. The SBC has sent 53,000 missionaries abroad from our Christian churches. We have about 85,000 at home and abroad. Why do they go? They really believe the Bible. They believe men and women will perish if they die without hearing the Gospel. There is a young preacher with four children who will leave the comfort of a wonderful church to go overseas to an Asian country. He believes God's call and commission is mandated through the Great Commission. To him, it is personal. It is authorized by the Scripture. He knows that he and his family will be protected by the Author of the Scriptures.

II. THIS LEADS US FROM THE AUTHORITY OF THE SCRIPTURE TO THE ACTIVITY OF THE SCRIPTURE

1. 2 Tim.3:16, "All Scripture is profitable for doctrine." It is not our task to try to prove, nor defend the Bible.

**We would be like Archie Bunker who was arguing religion with "Meathead." His son-in-law. Archie gets so frustrated he yells towards the kitchen: "Edith, get in here and help me defend God against this atheist." If Archie Bunker is God's defender, God doesn't have a chance.

The same holds true for you and me. We are not God's defenders. We are to be His spokesmen, His mouthpiece. I had another minister from another denomination to tell me, "We don't speak for God. We are not to attempt to do that." And in all my years I thought God had been speaking to me and through me about His Word. Well, I think I will continue in my ignorance and believe that God speaks to me and speaks through me. That I am a vehicle through which He speaks to others about Himself and their needs. We are to tell others how God's Word has affected our own lives. Doctrine is teaching about God, about man with God, and about man without God. And it has a positive offer in redeeming the unredeemed.

2. The inerrant Bible is also "profitable for ... reproof." In its prophecy and in its proclamation, the Bible mirrors truth. It sheds light on the right, as well as shining on the wrong. "For the Word of God is quick, and powerful, and sharper than a two-edged sword, piercing even to the dividing asunder of soul and spirit...and is a discerner of the thoughts and intents of the heart." It is God's all-seeing X-RAY! The Bible dispels spiritual darkness. "Once I was lost, but now I am found, the Light of the world is JESUS."

3. The Bible is profitable...for correction." It informs. It transforms when you conform to its truth. When we stray, it is the gyro compass that brings us back to the true North. Back to God. Do you know that sin will keep you from the Bible? Do you know that the Bible will keep you from sin?

4. A fourth activity of the Bible is "Instruction in righteousness." These present days of moral filth, ungodliness and anti-godliness were predicted in the Bible. See 1 Tim.4:1-5 and 2 Tim. 3:1-5. Evolutionists and Humanists, and New Agers declare mankind is slowly, but surely making its way upward from the lowly amoeba to the monkey, and from the monkey to man, and from man to the mastery of his own soul and destiny. My Bible teaches me that man without Divine inspiration and instruction is not climbing upward toward Godlikeness, but downward into the sewer pits of hell. For affirmation of this truth, simply watch the TV or read the daily news of man's growing inhumanity to man, and man's ignorance of the Divine Word of God. Our context tells us in 2 Tim.3:13. "Evil

men and seducers shall wax worse and worse, deceiving and being deceived." Jesus declared, before He returns:

> Lawlessness will abound,
> Love will grow cold.
> And faith will be hard to find.

The Revelation describes the last state of a Christless civilization and calls it BABYLON!

True believers will not be shocked, nor short-circuited in their faith and faithfulness by the failure of unbelievers around them. We are told in 2 Tim.3:14, "But (you) continue in the things (of God) which thou has learned and been assured of knowing of Whom thou hast learned them." By "Instruction," you are to plant your feet solidly on the solid Rock of Ages. You may sometimes tremble while you stand on the Rock, but the Rock shall never tremble beneath your feet.

I. The Authority of the Word.

II. The Activity of the Word, and Finally,

III. THE APPLICATION OF THE WORD

1. "That the man of God (believer) may be perfect, thoroughly furnished unto all good works." 2 Tim.3:17. The NIV translates: "That the man of God may be thoroughly equipped for every good work."

Does the Bible have the power to transform and bring triumph where evil and failure are enthroned?

**Let me give you just one event out of history. Remember Mutiny on the Bounty? By Robert Louis Stevenson. It is true story based on a ship, captained by Captain Bligh, on its way to Tahiti in search of the bread-fruit plants in the West Indies. Returning from Tahiti, the ship's crew tired of the ruthless Captain Bligh. They mutinied and put Captain Bligh and seventeen of his men adrift on a raft. The mutineers sailed back to Tahiti and went to the island Pitcairn. They stripped the ship Bounty and burned it. The sailors then started living a life of revelry and drunkenness. Within 10 years, all the fifteen mutineers were dead, except John Adams. Adams saw the desperate plight of the widows and children; he felt a responsibility towards them. John Adams found an old Bible in Captain Bligh's trunk. Adams began to read it. It transformed his life. He taught the Bible to the children. When the British government sent officers to arrest and punish any of the mutineers, they found a peaceful community with a church built by Adams, used as both school and church. Adams used only the Bible as his textbook. Today Pitcairn has a modern school. They need no police and have no jails. All this made possible by the transforming power of God's Book, the Bible. Captain Bligh's Bible is preserved and revered by people on the island today.

CONCLUSION

Last eve I passed beside a blacksmith's door, and heard the anvil ring the vesper chime. Then, looking in, I saw upon the floor old hammers, worn with the beating years of time. "How many anvils have you had," said I, "To wear and batten all these hammers so?" "Just one," said he, and then with twinkling eye, "The anvil wears the hammers out, you know." And so, thought I, the anvil of God's Word, for ages skeptic blows have beat upon. Yet, though the noise of falling blows was heard, the anvil is unharmed the hammers gone.
–Anonymous

"The church is a clinic on a mission for Christ."

THE HOLY GHOST REPAIR SERVICE

John 16:7-13

1. Out in Hollywood, California, there is an organization called "The Holy Ghost Repair Service." These are not Christians running a shoe repair business. Nor are they automobile mechanics.

On their stationary is their goal and stated purpose: "REPAIRING BROKEN LIVES FOR JESUS"

    —I like the ring of that purpose,
    —I like its promise,
    —I like its audacity.

This group of Christians has a street ministry reaching prostitutes, drug addicts and homeless people.

**Bobby and Dot Chance left Dallas, Texas, to go to Hollywood with a burning passion for down and outers, homeless people, and other cast-offs of society. Someone said this about them: "They dug a foxhole in the Devil's front yard."

2. It is my belief that the church of Jesus Christ is intended to be, and must be a Holy Ghost Repair Service. We cannot presume to be a church museum displaying perfect specimens of humanity. We are to be Christian clinics, on mission for Christ in an outreach ministry for broken spirits and lost souls. If we are not that, we do not deserve to be called a Christian body. We are here to tell everybody "God loves you." No matter if they are considered to be winners or losers in life. Whether they are down and outs, or up and outs, each person needs Jesus Christ internally and eternally. (Read John 16:7-13)

3. Everybody loves a winner. Most men, and a few women, enjoy watching a football receiver catch a ball and scurry across the goal line, watch him spike the football, raise his hands towards Heaven in thanksgiving to God for his moment of victory. We share in his enthusiasm.

** How many of you have heard of Roy Reigels? He played football for California. In the 1929 Rose Bowl, California was playing Georgia Tech. Tech's Stumpy Thomason fumbled the football and Roy Reigels picked it up and headed for the goal line. Headed for the wrong goal. Teammate Benny Lom stopped Reigels at the one-yard line. Tech players downed him there. Georgia Tech went on to win the game 8 points to 7. Roy Reigels was dubbed "Wrong Way Reigels." At halftime, He would have become overwhelmed with his mistake had his coach not taken the time to tell him it was OK. "You were out there busting your butt for the team. You were not the only one who made mistakes. Now we're a team and you are a part of it. Get out there the second half and show the fans what kind of football player you really are." What I am saying is this: In some way we are all losers, and fall short by our human mistakes. Yet the Lord loves us anyhow. And I think it is easier for Him to love a humble loser than it is to love an overly proud winner? Maybe!

4. We all live in a Humpty Dumpty world. And we all have fallen at one time or another. Now get this: We come to church searching and seeking a healing for our struggling spirits. That is, most of us do. And we need to find forgiveness from both God and man. We want reconciliation with the Lord and we want resolution with fellow church members. To me, the height of negativism is a church member who uses a brother's brokenness as a mirror to criticize him, and to display his own self-righteousness.

There is a real problem for the person who comes to church filled with so much egotism and "stuff" of the world, that he has no room for spiritual virtue and values. These people come to church empty, and they go away empty. Yes, empty at church! They show up at worship expecting very little, and they get it every time. There are some other church members who come to worship and they only have faith in their faith. And if that is all they've got, it falls short of personal fellowship with Jesus Christ.

— That is why you can hear some church members swearing.
— That is why you can see some church members cheating.
— That is why you can find so many church members happily mixing with a world that knows not God!

They are phonies! The Bible word is "Hypocrite" They might have a dose of religion. But religion without repentance creates more emptiness. And knowledge without obedience is a faith nobody needs. These up and outers need to understand this has been an age-old problem that reaches back into the days when our Lord Jesus Christ was resident on this earth. In the sixth chapter of John you can find religious people who were disconnected from God. Even in the Temple among the leadership. And for some of them, they knew they were not fulfilled in their temple attendance. Yet they saw something in Jesus Christ that caused them to want to change. Look at John 6, verse 2: "A great multitude followed Christ because they saw His miracles," which He did for those people who were diseased. The Holy Ghost Repair Service was at work among them.

**I had a preacher friend who told me the day of miracles belonged to that time and place when Jesus walked the earth. I did not argue with, nor dispute this good man. Although I knew, oh how I knew of God's healing power in my own family.

Let me tell you about a modern miracle 50 years in the making. My mother had ulcerated sores on her ankles for more than 50 years. She had tried medicines prescribed by many doctors. She had undergone removal of some veins in surgery to no avail. Every day and every night she changed bandages on her ankles. She lived in Belton, S.C. And during one of her episodes of pain and much personal discomfort, she became depressed. But I want to tell you the Holy Ghost repair service was at work! Marcia McCalister was the wife of Mama's doctor. She would drop by Mama's house two or three

51

times a week to visit and share lunch with her. One day she came by and saw my Mama's pain and despair. Marcia was a member of an Episcopal church. She asked Mama, "Mrs. Burton, do you believe in Divine Healing?" And my mother responded, "Of course." "Will you let me make an appointment to see my priest and let him pray for you? He has a gift for getting people healed." Mama's first response was, "What will your husband say about that?" "Never mind what he would say, will you go?" My Mom responded, "Yes." Two or three days later Marcia took Mama for her prayer appointment.

Now listen to me, the Holy Ghost repair service was at work, working through Marcia McCalister and through that priest. My mother went into the appointment so depressed and in so much pain. The priest prayed for her. She came from that experience with a smile on her face, and she knew she was on her way to healing. Next day she became a social being once again. My wife, Geraldine, had an every Friday commitment to my mother. They went from Due West to Belton, and on to Anderson where they would get their hair done. They would eat lunch together and go shopping for groceries. Dear soul, let me say to you who are feeling empty inside:

> If you think God is inactive,
> If you have not been plugged in to His power,
> If you have not witnessed His healing,
> then, let me tell you something.

The next Friday Mama told Geraldine she wanted to show her something. She unwrapped her bandages and there, where raw flesh had been an ongoing sore for fifty years, Geraldine saw some white and yellow "stuff" encircling her sores. God had commanded those white corpuscles to begin to overcome the diseased ankles. And within a few weeks my mother's legs were completely healed. And they stayed healed until she died on Jan.18,
1983. Eight years after her miraculous healing.

5. In John 5:6, the great Physician, asked a man afflicted for 38 years, "Wilt thou be made whole?" Of course the man wanted healing. He

had come to that place most every day for many years seeking to be healed. In John 5:8,
"Jesus saith unto him, 'Rise up and walk.'" And he did, to the astonishment of the people, and to the chagrin of Temple leaders. That crowd saw there was something most unusual about this Man, Jesus. And because of their own spiritual brokenness, they wanted to see more and to learn more.

6. In John 6:5-13 Jesus shows people another dimension of His grace when He feeds over 5,000 people from just a small bagful of bread and fish. Once again the Holy Ghost Repair Service is actuated through that young man and his lunch. ("A little becomes a lot when God is in it.") Do you see it? Because Jesus was God, He could cause the wheat to germinate, to be harvested, winnowed , ground into flour and made into bread. That is a miracle when you think about it. That is the natural way. Yet on any day, the Lord can by-pass natural laws and give piping hot rolls straight from the ovens of Glory. He sent manna from Heaven to feed Israel in the wilderness. But hear this warning: Things, produced by God and freely given to one and all, does not guarantee to satisfy that inner thirst and hunger that is deep within our spirits. Some dissatisfied souls get the idea "If only I had a few more things (toys), than I presently have, I would be satisfied and happy." They reach out to get more things and find they are still unfulfilled and still unhappy. They have been duped by the modern hype, "He who has the most toys, wins." Another wrong concept, "If I just had a change of scenery, I could move to Timbuktu, then I would have a better chance of being happy and fulfilled." But would you? <u>Places and things</u> won't satisfy your inner longings. What if you moved to one of the most desirable places in the U.S.A.? How about Mill Valley in California? That place is overflowing with affluence. Houses cost a million dollars and up. Driveways are filled with Mecedes, Winnebagos and large boats. Those people in Mill Valley have it made with all their luxury and security.

Tom Sine, in his book, <u>Why Settle for More and Miss the Best?</u> tells us, "In those fabulous homes are one of the highest levels of drug and alcohol abuse in our nation."

—Teen suicides and family break-ups are common and critical problems.
—This segment of society is a testimony that pleasure and treasure are not the answers to that missing element within all of us.

**Chuck Colson, the former "hatchet man" for Richard Nixon, told Christian Century magazine about his life before he met Jesus Christ as his personal Saviour. "I had arrived at everything I had ever dreamed of as a kid. I was 41 years old, had a healthy six-figure law practice with clients waiting at the door, a yacht in Chesapeake Bay, and a limousine and a driver. I was a friend to the President, and I had all kinds of people working for me...And I never felt more rotten in all my life."

And he remained with that feeling of rottenness until he talked with a friend who gave him good advice and a Christian book to read. This led him out of his misery to the Master. He found Jesus Christ as Saviour, and he found the real reason for his being on earth when he got personally involved in a prison ministry.

7. The good news of God's grace is that God is with us—
even when we lose,
even when we are sick.
even when we suffer loss.
even when we experience grief.
even when we simply fail.
If we will allow Him, God will teach us through our losses.
Comfort us when we sorrow.
Love us when we fail,
Save us in our lostness.

8. Are you here today and you are one of those disappointed, defeated church members? Do you have a desire to change? Are you ready for a spiritual makeover?

CONCLUSION

The Holy Ghost Repair Service has been active in this church today. The music, the prayers, the Word of God opened, the Holy Spirit working — all united to heal your brokenness, to strengthen your weakness. The Holy Spirit is now whispering to your soul to reach up and ask God to fill your spiritual needs.

He is calling for you to find Jesus Christ as your personal Saviour.
His call is for you to forsake the sin that now enslaves you.
He is calling for you to follow Him to perfect freedom.

And this keeping power will not be your own reliability, but it does give you access to His resources.

**A little girl had been taken to the hospital with a rare disease. She was given tablets to stop the disease from spreading. But she died there in the hospital. Her doctors were very disappointed, because the prescribed medicines had been working in similar cases. When the maid cleaned the child's room after her death, she found pills that had been thrown into an air vent. The child had thrown away the remedy for a restored life.

The Healer is here today. He is ready to give you what you most need. Don't turn your back on Him again and walk away. To do this is to deny yourself God's healing power for your soul. Amen!

"There are times when backing up is the best kind of progress."

<u>OLD TIME RELIGION</u>

Jude 3-8

I read these words and wondered:
"Today America is materially rich, but
morally rotten."

<u>But</u>, evolution says, "Man is ever progressing onward and upward."
New Ageism says we are to subvert our wills and purify ourselves
into becoming gods. Yet, our Lord Jesus warns that before He
returns: Lawlessness will abound, Love will abate. And faith will
be almost non-existent in high places.
                    -Vance Havner

Compare the above and tell me who is correct.

    Tell me: Why is there so much poverty in the midst of plenty?
    Why do we allow racial hatred to build walls of separation?
    Why is there so much crime? Unbelievable crime among
        families.
    Why do civilized people promote the killing of the unborn?
    Why do we pay professional athletes more in 1 year than we
        pay schoolteachers in a lifetime?

I'll tell you why: What modern man calls Progress is little more than
mighty efforts to build an earthly kingdom without God and without
righteous ethics. There are times when backing up is the best progress. And I am talking about backing up to the good old days and the
good old truths that dominated "old time religion" preaching.

Of course there are some things in "The good old days" that I don't
want to see again.

—**I don't** want to live in darkness without electricity.

—**I don't** want to walk to an outside toilet in the wintertime, nor even in the summertime. If Jack Frost does not bite you in the winter, certain bugs and spiders will get to you in the summer.

—**I don't** want to watch my two younger brothers have pneumonia, and the only treatment was a mustard poultice, and hear the doctor say to my family, "Tonight will be the turning point for either life or death." Meaning: Tomorrow morning they will be improved, or they will be dead.

—**I never** want to sleep in a cold room again where the wind blew its coldest breath through cracks in the walls and windows. Insulation for walls and ceilings was not available in those olden days.

But there were some solid values in the good old days: No one had to demand respect and fight for his rights. There was genuine respect for all people. There was a caring concern for your neighbors. No one locked their doors at night; nor when they were away for a day. There was a common sense of dignity and decency. And we did not learn that in school. We learned it from parents and grandparents. Parents did not have to worry where their children were at nighttime. They were at home. And children did not have to worry about where their parents were at midnight.

You see. There were rigid rules, mainly unwritten that regulated our society. And that social agenda was the outgrowth of what I will now call, **"The Old Time Religion."**

Not everybody was religious - but everybody lived with a healthy respect for Christian people and Christian values. Attending church was one of the biggest events of the week.

WHAT WAS THE OLD TIME RELIGION?

-It was a creed to be kept. It was a doctrine to be believed. It was a faith that always evoked faithfulness to God and His church. And all these virtues spilled over into our schools and communities. You were very careful to do nothing that would bring blame and shame upon family or God's church. Here is what the "Old time Religion" taught:

I. THAT THE BIBLE IS THE TRUE WORD OF GOD AND IS RELIABLE

In: Conviction of disabling sin.
     Conversion of the soul.
         Consistent Christian living.
             Committed service to God and man.
                Comforting to the saints.
                   Connecting time with
                   eternity.

And from what I have heard and read of the old days, nobody walked away from a church service uncertain about their future. THEY KNEW they were either Heaven-bound or Hell-bound.

The saved had a destiny with God in Heaven.
The unsaved had a destiny with Satan in Hell.

II. THEY ALSO PREACHED ABOUT A LIVING MONSTER AND ENEMY CALLED THE DEVIL.

That he is a constant home wrecker and soul destroyer. That he goes "about this earth seeking whom he may devour." People in those days did not excuse, nor blame their sinfulness on their parents, nor on poor upbringing. They believed it and they preached it, that there is a powerful, evil spirit who can woo and win, tease and tempt. One who will control anyone who is not controlled by the Lord. Modern man has laughed at the possibility of such a spirit. They have denied his personage and power. And because of that, they blame the gone-wrongness of man on imperfect genes and chromosomes.

But listen to Alfred J. Hough summation of that denial:

"Men don't believe in the devil now, as their fathers used to do.
They've forced the door of the broadest creed to let his majesty
    through.
There isn't a print of his cloven foot, or fiery dart from his bow
To be found on earth or air today, for the world has voted it so.

Who dogs the steps of the toiling saint and digs the pit for his
    feet?
Who sows the tares in the fields of time whenever God sows His
    wheat?
The devil is voted not to be, and of course the thing is true.
But who is doing the kind of work that the devil alone can do?"

We're told that he doesn't go about as a roaring lion now;
But whom shall we hold responsible for the everlasting row
To be heard in the home, in church and state, to the earth's
    remotest bound.
If the devil by unanimous vote is nowhere to be found?

Won't someone step to the front and show
How the frauds and crimes of this day spring up, we want to
    know.
The devil was fairly voted out, and of course the devil's gone,
But simple people would like to know, who's carrying his busi-
    ness on?"

Preachers of the Old Time Religion knew, and true preachers of the
Word today know who he is. He is the one whom Jesus called "a liar
and a deceiver." He was and he still is.

Have you ever heard a confused and hurting person ask, "Why did
God do this to me?" No real answer because it is a false question.
The correct question, is, "Why did Satan do this to me?"

Satan is a former archangel whose name was Lucifer. He stood
among the heights of Heaven, and made the eternal mistake of
coveting the majesty and glory of God. And because of this sin he

fell to the pits of ongoing evil. Now he is trying to doom every soul to hell with him. You must remember, and always know that he is your enemy, and he is a master deceiver.

III. THIRDLY, THE OLD TIME RELIGION PREACHED THAT HELL IS HOSTILE AND HOT.

It is the eternal dwelling place of the unsaved. These devoted preachers could almost tell you the temperature in that damnable furnace of the doomed. One old timer: "I once saw molten red hot lava flowing from a live volcano. They use that for ice cream in that place of lost souls." ─-Jesus compared hell to the burning garbage dump outside the walls of Jerusalem, and it was called "Gehenna." It was a place of filth, a place of fire, a place of final futility.

Yet, some modern preachers have taken hell out of their sermons, leading their hearers to have false hopes. "How can a loving God allow a human soul to go to such an awful place?" Why don't they ask this question, "Why would a loving God allow unredeemed killers, devil worshipers, liars and rapists of little girls into Heaven?" To let them make Heaven into a hell?

My question is to the unredeemed: "Why will any person refuse to receive the pardon and grace of God that will open the gates of Heaven for them?" In Heaven I would not want to live next door to an unredeemed, cussing sailor. You would not want to live next door to an unredeemed murderer. On earth we have to separate people in society from one another. We must separate the lawbreakers from law abiders. Law abiders can live anywhere they desire. Lawbreakers must be incarcerated from good people who keep the laws of God and the ethics of man.

But we have a compromising lawyers and judges who would unlock every prison to let criminals live in your community. They'll never do that, and they'll never open the gates of Hell for evil men and women to overrun Heaven. Nor will they be able to negotiate to construct air conditioners in the ovens of eternity.

Thus, there is separation and protection for the unlawful here. There is separation and punishment for the unsaved hereafter. And once a person goes there, it is a capital sentence, he will never be able to leave.

IV. THE OLD TIMERS ALSO PREACHED THAT HEAVEN IS DESIRABLE, SWEET AND SECURE.

Once you get there, you'll never want to move to some other place. And for the inhabitants, there will be no more problems. No more pain. No more heartbreak. No more hatred. No more disappointments. No more disasters. No more warring. No more worrying.

Saints love to sing: There's a land that is fairer than day,
And by faith we can see it afar.
For the Father waits over the way,
To prepare us a dwelling place there.
In the sweet by and by, we shall dwell on that beautiful shore.

And brother, if that hope does not stir your soul, then your stirrer is broken. If that thought does not warm your heart, you need God's type of heart transplant.

V. ONE FINAL THING: THE PREACHERS OF YESTERDAY PREACHED THAT THE TIME TO BE SAVED IS SHORT

Time is never the ally of a person who is walking away from the Lord. In the olden days there were church bells that rang, calling believers to worship.

**One lad went horse riding one Sunday with his buddies. While riding, they heard the church bells ringing in the distance. This lad told the others, "I'm going back while I can still hear the church bells."

It is time for some of you to turn back to God's code of conduct that was once preached, believed and lived in the "Old Time Religion" days. Return now "to the faith which was once delivered to the saints." Jude 3b   Amen.

"People of this world are troubled and sin-sick because they have walked with muddy feet on God's sacred soil."

HOLY GROUND

Exodus 3:1-5

Pity the person who has never stood with God on Holy Ground.

1. Moses did at Mt. Horeb, and we are allowed to share in this sacred moment as we read Exodus 3:1-5

2. The Apostle Peter did on the Mount of Transfiguration, and he gives this testimony in 2 Peter 1:16-18

3. People of this world are troubled and sin-sick this very day because they have walked with muddy feet on God's sacred soil, and the key to their problem is defined in Romans 3:18, "There is no fear of God before their eyes."

— In this world of guided missiles and misguided men, man is smart enough to split the unsplittable atom, but he is not wise enough to be entrusted with this immense power.

— In this age of technology, some of our progress may not be real progress after all. In the Stone Age men fought and killed with bows and arrows. In the Space Age we kill with bullets and bombs. Is that the kind of progress we want?

4. Beloved, when people, and nations, take their eyes off God and put them onto something else, they stumble and fall. And that collapse can be felt among generations all over the world. Remember Russia? A great land of faith and promise before atheism took it over. Some great art and inspiring music of deep faith were created in that land that fell into the hands of God's enemy. Any person, or nation, who takes their eyes off God, has the capacity to slip into moral filth.

When people take their eyes off the Lord: Eternal things become blurred. Motives become self-seeking. Human wills become overmastered with secondary values.

**Elizabeth Barrett Browning caught a glimpse of God's Glory and stood on Holy Ground when she wrote: "Earth's crammed with heaven,

> And every common bush afire with God
> But only he who sees takes off his shoes,
> The rest sit round and pluck blackberries."

5. May the dear Lord help us in this worship hour to stop what we are doing and thinking, to stand firm with Him on Holy Ground. Teaching us how to live holy among unholy men.

I. PETER, JAMES AND JOHN DID THAT DAY AT MT. HEBRON

1. What a glorious experience when God allowed these three earthbound men to see His glory. It opened their eyes. It sobered their confused minds. It blessed their doubting hearts. It stopped their whining and criticizing... All because they took time to witness the glory of Jesus Christ, their Leader and Redeemer. They now had it confirmed that He was God's promised Saviour of all who would believe. Son of man, without besetting sin. Son of God with immense power. He was God's Remedy for the world's tragedy, the Answer for all human doubt and dilemma.

2. Beloved it is up to you. Don't allow yourself to be overwhelmed with the secular society that excludes God from our schools, our government, and even excluding Him from their homes.

— If you have been overcome by the temptations of the times,
— If you have drunk from the fountains of foolishness, and you still thirst,
— If you have fed on ashes, and you are still spiritually hungry,
— If you come to the church empty and go away empty,

I want to tell you that you can be set free. That you can begin your journey out of the ash heaps to stand with God and His church on His mountain of purity and power. It can happen for you this very hour.

** Let's begin together by following the advice in Helen Lemmel's song:

"Turn your eyes upon Jesus, look full in His wonderful face.
And the things of earth will grow strangely dim,
in the light of His Glory and grace."

> PAUSE FOR PRAYER: "Lord, we're tired of walking alone in our spiritual journey. We're tired of trying to do Your work with limited human strength. We need more than we've got. Come into my heart with fullness this very moment, O Holy Spirit. Empower me to stand with You in every way, and every day on Your Holy Ground. I ask this in the name of Jesus, Your Son, Who is my Saviour and Lord. Amen."

(Yes, you can stop talking to people for a moment in order to talk to God)

If you prayed this prayer in sincerity, you'll begin to see things, people and circumstances, as you've never seen them before.

— You will come to church filled with glorious expectations.
— You will hear God's voice through singing and praying, testimony and sermon.
— You'll hear the melody of angels in hymns of praise,
— You'll see your fellowman as Divine potential with God; yet, in peril without Him.
— You'll even see yourself differently, an object of God's Divine love and grace.

The Lord is always speaking to us through circumstances that happen to us, ever trying to draw us onto Holy and Healing Ground with Him.

**It happened to Brenda and Jerry Connors who live in Connecticut. Their marriage was falling apart after eight years and two children. They argued constantly over trivial things. They agreed to get a divorce after Jerry found work nearer home. He worked in New York City. But he could not find work in their town. Economic problems kept them under one roof. Brenda was so distraught and desparate, she started attending a weekly prayer service at an Episcopal church in a near by-town. This increased her misery. (She probably saw her own shortcomings) One night, the couple had a terrible verbal fight. Jerry went to the bedroom and locked the door. Brenda thought about leaving with the children. However, next morning she drove away, not knowing where to go. She ended up in Darien, at the same Episcopal Church. She went in. The rector, whom she had not met, selected John 14, and he talked about the Holy Spirit as Comforter. Then he said, "The Lord is moving in this place today. Some person is here whose marriage is breaking up. And God wants to heal the relationship. So I am telling you, let go and let God." Brenda did! She yielded her spirit to the Lord. Back home, amid unusual quietness, they had lunch. Jerry spoke, "A strange thing happened today while you were gone. Something told me to find a Bible. It took me a while to find yours. I opened it and started reading in John 14, about the Holy Spirit helping us..."You know the rest of the story. They both moved out of their human weakness onto God's foundation of strength; Forgiveness, renewal, restoration! Healing!

Brenda's own word: "Today, the marriage I thought was beyond repair, is stronger than ever." <u>Hallelujah!</u>

God can do it for anybody who is willing to plug in to His holy, healing, enabling power.

3. If you are here today and you need the Lord's touch. He knows you. He knows your situation. He knows your need, and He is ready now to supply that need. I invite you to step onto Holy Ground with the Father, and allow Him to administer His grace and healing to your heart. "Casting all your care upon Him, for He careth for you." I Peter 5:7

For Brenda and Jerry Connors it was a wonderful life-changing, problem-solving experience. Now they can say with the Apostle Peter: "We were eye-witnesses of His majesty." And it continues to happen when you ask Jesus to take control of your life.

II. AND FROM THAT HOLY GROUND EXPERIENCE, PETER HAD IT CONFIRMED IN HIS HEART WHAT HE ALREADY BELIEVED ABOUT JESUS CHRIST.

1. Back in Matt.16:13b, Jesus had asked His disciples, "Whom do men say that I am?" They responded, "John the Baptist," "Elias, or one of the prophets." "But whom do YOU say that I am?" Verse 16: Peter spoke up and said, "Thou art the Christ, the Son of the living God."

2. There are far too many saved people who are just barely on the inner edge of faith.

** It is like they're still at the train station where they first arrived for salvation. They do believe that Jesus Christ is the son of man through Mary. They believe He is the Son of God Jehovah. However, because they are only on the inner edge of faith, sometimes it takes a movement of God for them to take a leap of faith into the inner circle of intimate fellowship with God and fellow believers.

**Even then, it might happen that such an experience is not enough to keep Simon Peter from denying Christ when the time of testing comes. It didn't keep Peter from returning back to his fishing nets after Jesus was crucified. If Jesus is allowed to diminish in your heart, you, too, are vulnerable to future disappointments. When your faith wavers a bit, just keep looking to Jesus. He will come to you.

3. And even though Peter had stood on Holy Ground with Christ, it still took two other facets of faith to change him from a rascal to a rock.

FIRST: It was the resurrection of Jesus Christ. The Cross had defused their enthusiasm. And it was after Jesus rose from the dead that Peter felt the fire of faith burning again in his soul. It seems that most of Christ's early disciples thought they had connected with a failure when Jesus died on the Cross. But their faith was rekindled when He came forth from the grave. No one can remain defeated when Christ is in his presence. NO ONE!

SECOND: The second facet of faith that energized Peter's feeble and failing faith, was the coming of the Holy Spirit. He gave them needed power to live the Christian life. He gave them a penetrating witness to share the Good News. It is impossible to become what God intends for you to be without Holy Spirit anointing.

Now all the disciples knew, that in Jesus, the present valley of sadness and scorn and despair was only temporary. Ahead for them was ultimate victory in the Lord. Friday is here, but Sunday's a'coming!

** Remember the fiery furnace in Daniel 3? Three men, Shadrach, Meshach and Abednego were thrown into the firey furnace by King Nebuchadnezzar. And when people looked into the furnace they saw four people walking in the flames. The fourth figure was the Lord! How many men were thrown into the furnace? And how many came out? Three cast in, and three came walking out of the flames. This indicates to me that my Lord is still in there with me in the fires of trouble. And He will be there for you when you are troubled.

Beyond the heartaches, Peter knew there was hope and healings. Beyond the grave there is life eternal to every believer. And, knowing that, really knowing that is true, the Lord will put a song in your heart. He will put a testimony on your lips, with service to God among your highest priorities. I repeat: Pity the person who has never stood with God on Holy Ground.

We turn now to the final observation of Peter's Holy Ground experience.

III. PETER DISCOVERED WHAT REAL MINISTRY IS ALL ABOUT

1. Look again at Matt. 17:4. Peter wants to live forever in the presence of Jesus, with God speaking directly to them out of the clouds. This is heavenly. This is oneness and closeness to God, the Father. Peter was ready to set up permanent headquarters there in the hills with Jesus, Moses and Elijah. Wouldn't that be a happy day?

Peter still persisted, "Lord, it is good for us to be here." And it was! Christian love and sweet fellowship. We enjoy getting apart from swearing crowds and turmoils of temptations.

**Johnson Oatman's song is the expression of our hearts:

> "I'm pressing on the Upward Way;
> New heights I'm gaining every day.
> Still praying as I onward bound,
> Lord plant my feet on higher ground.
> I want to live above the world, tho Satan's darts at me are hurled,
> For (MY) faith has caught the joyful sound,
> The song of saints on HIGHER GROUND"

2. To me, it is heavenly to be seated in this sanctuary together with brothers and sisters in Christ. This special place is a sanctuary from the world that denies my God. It is a refuge, a little corner of Heaven. Sad to say, for those unwilling to walk with God on Holy Ground, this hour and this place is little more than a prison on Sunday morning. They come expecting nothing and get it every time. To them, the most exciting part of the service is the benediction. They are pathetic people who are stuck in religiosity. The same yesterday, today and tomorrow!

3. Peter thought about setting up a commune, housekeeping. Erect walls to keep worldlings out. To sit round and share those blackberries Elizabeth Barrett wrote about. Just sitting and waiting for Christ's coming for us, or our going to be with Him.

71

4. But think about this — what if our ancestors had done this? Who would have gone outside the walls to witness and to win lost souls for Jesus? Where would you be had no one taken time to share the Christian faith with you? Just imagine what would have resulted if Peter, James and John had set down roots and stayed on that Mount that transfigured their thinking.

—There would have been no Pentecost where thousands of people were reached by the Lord through the Apostle Peter.
—There would have been no epistles of John, James and Peter.
—There would be no ongoing mission effort to warn the world about coming destruction, and no one to witness redemption through Jesus Christ. You would be as the pagan, trying to please an unknown god. You could be Muslim, with designs to kill all who would not accept your futile faith.

5. Do you see it? Yes, go to the mountains with God, you need it. Don't ever pass up a chance to stand with God on Holy Ground. But you must remember this, the earthly mission of Jesus Christ was not in the hills with chosen friends, but down in the valley where a hurting humanity was lost and suffering. And if your faith does not reach beyond these four walls, then your faith is fruitless and unfulfilling.

The fact is, as soon as Christ and His disciples moved down the mountains, they met a man in misery. His son was epileptic and needed Christ's touch and healing. All people do!

CONCLUSION

The reason so many Christian's faith is empty and incomplete, is because it seems when they go out the church door, they leave their faith behind. They missed the opportunity to stand with the Lord on Holy Ground. They walked away without hearing His holy commands and purpose for their life.

** A man came rushing into a church one morning. And he asked, "What time does the service begin?" An usher told him, "Worship begins in five minutes. The service begins when you walk back out of those doors."

Let me ask you, and you, and you. Are you a spectator? Or, are you a participant in what God is trying to do in this world? In this community? In this church? I invite you to step onto Holy Ground with God this morning if you have never done it before. And when you do, you'll never be the same again. Amen!

"The church that Christ came to build must be a lighthouse on a hill, radiating and penetrating into spiritual darkness where lost souls abide."

THE SUPREME TASK OF THE CHURCH

Acts 20:17-24

1. "What is the greatest business in the world?"

**A preacher began his sermon with that question. For emphasis, he repeated the question again. A little boy sitting on the front pew responded, "Potato chips." People laughed, but most everybody in the congregation knew why he said that. His father was in the potato chip business.

2. No doubt, I think you will agree that the greatest business in the world is our Heavenly Father's business.

3. Read Acts 20:17-24. And verse 24 is God's mission that becomes our mission, "To testify the Gospel of the grace of God." This is the supreme task of the church. And as a member of God's church, how do you react to this task? If you are saved, you become God's Light to anybody and everybody who dwells in spiritual darkness. That is my task, the deacon's task, and it is your task as well. You become God's love to show the unlovely that God really cares for them. He cared enough to give His only Begotten Son to save them from sin and eternal destruction, and to provide for them an eternal home in glory with Him.

> Christ has no hands but our hands to do His work today.
> He has no feet but our feet to lead men in His way.
> He has no tongue but our tongue to tell men how He died.
> He has no help but out help to bring them to His side.
> —Annie Johnson Flint

4. And if you think the church is only a place to check in for Brownie points with God, you are already falling far short of God's expectations for yourself, in His ongoing ministry to reach the unreached for His Kingdom.

**Early one evening TV channel 12 in Augusta announced that three little boys were missing in North Augusta. A couple had moved into a home in North Augusta that day. A cousin was playing with the two sons while mom and dad were busy getting their furniture into their new house. Night had fallen, and the three boys were missing. Several hundred people responded to the appeal for help. About 200 of us marched side by side through some dense woods and under-brush behind the home. I saw strong men and weak men marching together. White people and black people, Praying people and swearing people, Sober people, and two or three had been drinking alcohol. All united in the search for three lost children. The boys were not found early, so much of the crowd went home. About 2 or 3 AM we heard someone yell, "We have found them." The boys were about 75 yards in back of the home. They had crawled under a tree and covered themselves with pine needles to ward off the cold night air. What wonderful rejoicing by all the hunters.

This experience so moved me that I prepared a message for my flock on "Seeking the Lost." And I told them, "If the saved and the unsaved can unite to find 3 missing children, why can't the church, our church, unite effectively to reach the lost in this community for Jesus Christ?" I am still wondering about that. Listen church member! We are told in 2 Tim. 2:4, "We have been approved by God to be entrusted with the Gospel." There can be no options to this crucial mandate from the Lord.

5. So! There are four important revelations to consider in the "Church's Supreme Task" on this earth.

I. THE MAGNITUDE OF THE TASK

.

1. The church that Jesus came to build on earth must be a Lighthouse on a hill, radiating and penetrating into spiritual darkness where lost souls abide. <u>It is world-encompassing</u>. And God has appointed you, a redeemed soul, to go forth to share His love and Light to the unredeemed who live and work and play around in your environment. God has appointed you to share your faith with your lips. God has appointed you to prove your faith with your life, and He has empowered you to share His love by giving you a capacity to love the unloving.

Silence becomes sinful if we have a cure for a diseased and dying person, and we share it not. Genuine faith will always find a way to be faithful in witnessing to the unsaved in the name of the Lord Jesus Christ.

2. God will not call His church to do what He will not equip them to do. To become an effective part of God's ongoing outreach for the unreached, two very important things must happen.

a. You must be willing to develop a <u>passion for souls.</u> You must learn to love them, to pray daily for them, and to seek them with all your heart. Knowing that you may be the only person a lost neighbor or friend will listen to. This passion has to become a front burner, high priority love that puts first things first in your quest to serve the Lord. Think about it, there are some lost souls within your reach, and if you make no effort to win them to Christ and His church, they will probably die in their sins to be lost forever. If their house were burning down, would you warn them? Their soul is in desperate peril, are you willing to warn them?

**Daniel March wrote a challenging poem that Mozart set to music:

Hark the voice of Jesus calling, "Who will go and work today?"
Fields are white and harvests waiting,
who will bear the sheaves away?"
Loud and long the Master calleth, rich reward He offers free,
Who will answer, gladly saying, "Here am I, send me, send me?"

Let none hear you idly saying, "There is nothing I can do."
While the lost of earth are dying and the Master calls for you.
Take the task He gives you gladly; let His work your pleasure be,
Answer quickly when He calls you, "Here am I send me, send me."

2. If you are to undertake the magnitude of the task, you must see lost souls through the eyes of our Lord. Matt.9:36, "When (Jesus) saw the (lost) multitude, He was moved with compassion because they fainted, and were scattered abroad as sheep having no shepherd."

LOOK TO SEE WHAT HE SAW:

a. He saw their departure from God. "All we, like sheep, have gone astray." We have walked in unGodly ways. Isaiah 53:6

We have fellowshipped with unGodly people.
We have walked and stumbled in darkness.
We have wasted valuable time.

b. Jesus saw the multitude's depravity in sin; Born in sin. Living in sin, Dying in sin. And if no one reaches them for Jesus, eternity in sin is the result.

c. He saw their destiny in Hell. Where there is separation and suffering.

When you are willing to visualize this, you will partner with God in efforts to reach the unsaved around you. You are saved. You are saved to serve. The fruit of one Christian is another Christian. Jesus tells you in Matt.4:19, "Follow me and I will make you a fisher of men." (See I Cor.9:19-20) This is the way God is accomplishing the worldwide task of winning the lost, one person at a time.

II. THE APPEAL OF THE TASK

1. The appeal comes from above. 2 Cor.5:14,"The love of Christ constrains us." When Jesus looked at the lost multitude, He told His disciples, "The harvest is plenteous, but the laborers are few." — Do you understand what Jesus was saying to those disciples? Do you understand He is saying the same thing to us? He needs our help. He needs your help.

> The harvest time for souls is now ready.
> The laborers with a willingness to obey are few.
> The harvest is in jeopardy of perishing.
> Our time for harvesting is short.

Attention Church! Listen Christians! "As the Father hath sent me, so send I you." John 20:21

> God, the Father, needs your involvement.
> God, the Son, is depending on you to respond.
> God, the Holy Spirit, will enable you to witness to the unreached.

You can do something when you are willing to help. He will equip you, and use you when you volunteer and yield some special time for Him to use you.

2. The appeal also comes from beneath. Dives in Hell begged Abraham "Please go tell my five brothers not to come to his place of torment." How sad, a man already in Hell and he knew the rest of his family was on their way there. His family had neighbors and church members all around them who did not seem to care about their lostness.

**Beloved, just imagine you had been rescued from a sinking ship. You made it to the beach where you could do one of two things: (1)

Get on your knees and thank God for your deliverance, or (2) Get busy trying to throw lifelines out to others still struggling and still drowning in the deep waters. Which do you think God would prefer that you do? If you have been saved, should you not be busy at God's task to get others saved? The appeal still comes from above. And it still is echoing from beneath.

> I. The Magnitude of the Task.
> II. The Appeal of the Task.

III. THE RESPONSIBILITY FOR THE TASK (See Ezekiel 3:17-18)

There are three Imperatives for every Christian:

1. Responsibility - God has commissioned no agency outside the church to share His Gospel. But He has called His redeemed church members to be His witnesses locally, nationally and internationally. The very last words of our Lord to His church were in Acts 1:8, "Ye shall receive power after that the Holy Ghost is come upon you. And ye shall be witnesses unto me in Jerusalem, (here) and in all Judea (Your state), and in Samaria (USA) and unto the uttermost part of the earth."

You need to get involved with some plan to reach people everywhere on behalf of our Lord. You can get busy in all mission opportunities with your gifts and with your prayers. You can get involved in your going, in your work, where you live, and where you play.

2. Another imperative is Opportunity. Several hunters were eating an early breakfast in bear country. A big burly trucker about 6' 6" weighing about 300 pounds, came in and ordered breakfast. A small guy looked up at him in deep admiration. He told the trucker, "Man, if I was your size I would go out in them woods and find the biggest bear, and I'd tear him limb from limb." The big fellow looked at the small fellow and told him, "There's some bears out there that are your size, go out and get you one of them."

We are not expected to personally try to win Kings and Presidents. We do not have access to them. But we do have access to lost people all around us. On the same street where we live, in the same houses where we abide, at the same workplace where we work. Yes, we have all kinds of opportunities to witness to people we meet every day. When we are willing to witness, the Holy Spirit will cause our paths to cross with lost people needing a witness. It is not that we do not have opportunity to witness, we simply do not take sufficient time to witness.

**I was recently in a store that resells items for Habitat for Humanity. I talked briefly with a black lady who worked there. Then I left the store. Next morning she was dead. I don't know if she had saving faith. Had I taken the time I could have asked her. I didn't. <u>A Lost opportunity for me!</u>

3. Another imperative in becoming responsible for the task is Availability. God wants to take your littleness to show you His bigness. Tomorrow morning, will you be willing look in your mirror, and tell the Lord, "Today, I don't know how and I don't know who, but if there is somebody who needs to hear me say that You love them, dear God, please do it through me." It may not happen today. But it can never happen tomorrow until you are willing to let the Lord move through you right now.

**Adoniram Judson went to Burma as God's missionary. He worked and witnessed 7 years before he won his first convert to Christ.

**Martha Franks said it took her 7 years to win her first convert to Jesus in China. It took 15 years in Tahiti, 17 years in Bengali.

Responsibility for witnessing began yesterday. Fulfillment can begin today. Fruition will be evident tomorrow. The goal and the appeal of the mission is to begin working on one soul at a time. Are you willing?

IV. FAITHFULNESS LEADS TO THE REWARDS OF THE TASK

There is a promise in Ps. 126:5-6, "They that sow in tears shall reap in joy. He that goeth forth weeping shall doubtless come again with rejoicing. Bringing his sheaves with him."

** A nephew by marriage went on a mission trip to the islands in the Caribbean. I saw him after the trip, and he came up to me with a glow of glory in his eyes. He told me, "Uncle Wade, the day we landed I won my first convert to the Lord." He was so jubilant he won several more to Jesus on that trip that was designed to reach people for the Lord. Greater than any movie Oscar, greater than any olympic gold medal. Nothing you will ever do, or accomplish, can compare with your witnessing and winning a lost soul from the prison of enslaving sin to the paradise of God's salvation and safety. Dear saint of God. Please find someone who is unchurched and unsaved and lead that person to Jesus. Or, lead them to some other Christian who will lead them to Jesus. Look forward - Are you on your way to Heaven? Look backward, is there anyone following you to Heaven? That is our task as Christians. We need to get serious and to get involved in this task for God.

CONCLUSION

I heard the following story at an Evangelism Conference held in Charleston, S.C. many years ago. There was a Christian lady named Bo. She lived in Atlanta. Bo was a dedicated Christian. She was a consistent soul seeker and soul-winner. One day she asked her pastor, "Do you know a John Sheffield?" The pastor said, "I don't think I do." Bo told her pastor, "The Lord has put this name on my heart for prayer and salvation." She went to the church office to check the names of people listed as prospects for her church. No John Sheffield. Bo kept praying for John Sheffield. Bo's church prepared to go on a mission trip to Massachusetts. Bo volunteered to go. All that week they visited in homes, and Bo was expecting to meet John Sheffield. The last day for the mission work had come. The group gathered in the parking lot waiting for the bus to carry them back to Atlanta. Bo saw a house across the road, "Has anybody been to that house?" No. She asked another lady to go with her to the house. No one was at home. As they were headed back to the parking lot, a car pulled up to the curb and a man asked, "Is this the road to _____?" He named a port city. Bo, "I don't know, we are here on a visit from Georgia. By the way, my name is Bo." "Glad to meet you," said the man, "My name is Jack. Bo is an unusual name for a lady." "I know," said Bo, "My real name is Bonita." "And my real name is John," said the man. Bo looked at him and said, "You are John Sheffield." The man laughed and asked, "How did you know that?" Bo told him how the Lord had put his name on her heart to pray for his salvation. John Sheffield paled, and told them, "I need to be saved. I am on my way to catch a ship home to England to try to get my wife not to divorce me." There on the spot Bo led Sheffield to the Lord. After they had prayed, Bo took a New Testament from her purse and gave it to John. "Read what is written inside," said Bo. John read these words inscribed on the front page, "To John Sheffield on the day he accepted Jesus Christ as his personal Saviour." Amen!

FORSAKEN ON THE CROSS

Matt. 27:45-50

Up Calvary's Mountain, one dreadful morn,
Walked Christ my Saviour, weary and worn.

Facing for sinners, death on the Cross,
That He might save them from endless loss.
— Avis Christiansen

CALVARY — Where the holiest of all men prayed, while a
howling mob profaned the Son of God.

CALVARY — Where the Light of the world entered darkness,
that we, who were in darkness might come to
God's eternal Light.

CALVARY — Where the wrath of God was poured out upon
Jesus, that the mercy of God might be poured
out upon us.

1. Men at the Cross, and before the Cross, and since the Cross, have always been restricted by tunnel vision.

**Over 400 years ago a man named Copernicus shook the religious world by declaring the sun, and not the moon, was the center of gravity for our solar system. Churchmen of that day wanted to hang him for heresy. "Does not the Bible teach that the earth is four-cornered in Isaiah 11:12?" (It appeared that way from man's point of view) They overlooked Isaiah 40:22 that speaks of the "Circle of the earth." That is from God's point of view.

But Copernicus was wrong! Our sun is just a tiny speck in the Milky Way Galaxy of 2 billion other suns. Somewhere out there, perhaps in Orion, or the Pliades, known only to God, is the center of gravity, that vital force that does double duty in holding things together, while at the same time, it holds things apart.

2. I said all that to say this: There is a moral center of gravity in our world, and it is found only in Jesus Christ, the Son of the living God, the One Who created all things. In spite of this, man has tried with artificial human aids to solve complicated spiritual problems. And where systems have failed, where philosophies have failed, and where governments have failed, even religions have failed, Jesus Christ, God's only begotten Son has never failed. "In Him all things consist." Col.1:7 He is the moral balance that keeps our world from sinking into blind heathenism, humanism and atheism. He is God's "Lamb that was slain from the foundation of the world." Meaning: The Cross was not just an accidental event in the misguided happenings of man. Rather, the Cross was Providential planning for man's redemption in the loving heart of God.
God knew when Adam and Eve fell in sin that no man could ever redeem himself. For redemption costs a terrible price. It costs innocent life. It costs life-giving blood. "For without the shedding of blood, there is no remission for sin."Heb. 9:22

3. If life is to be maintained and ongoing, something has to die to sustain that life. You are living now because something died for you. The grain died to give you bread. The beans and potatoes died to give you carbohydrates and protein. The cattle have to die to give you meat. The death of one thing is necessary to sustain the life of another.

4. In the spiritual realm, Jesus, the Divine, had to die for man, if man is to live eternally. I Cor.15:3, "Christ died for our sins according to the Scriptures." Jesus became the Bread of Life to believers who would partake of His body by faith. He is the Water of Life to all who will drink from this eternal spring to sustain them.

5. Jesus was, and is, God's promised Redeemer. And if we are to get the truest picture of redemption from the Cross, we find it in Matt. 27:46. Listen again as Jesus speaks as He is dying on Golgotha:

"Eli, Eli, lama sa bach tha ni?" "My God, My God, why hast Thou forsaken me?" In these awesome moments of agony, Heaven earth shook in fury when the suffering Son of God cried out: In the temple nearby, the heavy veil between the Holy Place and the Holy of Holies is ripped asunder. And how was it ripped? V.51, "From the top to the bottom. Meaning God ripped apart that which separated mortal man from His holy Presence. From solid foundations even the rocks quiver and quake at the sound of His voice. From the home of the dead, graves open, and saints rise to be seen walking in the cities. V.52

6. V. 45, "Now from the sixth hour, there was darkness all over the land until the ninth hour." This would be noon until 3:00 PM. The light of the sun is eclipsed. It is night at noonday. The mockery of the crowd had ceased. A strange fear gripped their hearts. The silence is broken by the labored breathing and groaning of three men, slowly dying on three crosses.

7. Suddenly, from that mysterious darkness Jesus cried out, "My God, my God, why hast Thou forsaken me?" Was He quoting from Psalm 22? Was He begging for physical relief from His bitter agony?

** The German reformer, Martin Luther, questioned: "God forsaken of God? Who can understand it?"
** A holy man in India looked at the sun's eclipse and wrote in his journal: "Either God is suffering at this moment, or He is in deep sympathy with someone who is suffering."

This was the holy of holies of Christ's sufferings. Deeper and deeper He went into the valley of judgment for man's sin. Already He had prayed for His enemies, He had given assurance to a new believer, He had provided for His mother.

And now He leaves the earthly scene and enters God's Temple to become the sacrifice for sin and sinners. The Lamb goes to the sacrificial altar. Remember the apostle John speaking to the ages when he proclaimed: "Behold the Lamb of God that takes away the sin of the world."

8. Understand it fully, we cannot, but we can comprehend it in part. In this pitiful cry from the Cross that we see three primary truths:

> I. THE HUMANITY OF JESUS
> II. THE WRATH OF GOD AGAINST SIN
> III. THE GRACE OF GOD.

I. FIRST, THE HUMANITY OF JESUS

1. When Jesus cried out, "My God, my God," He was revealing His absolute identity with mankind. This is one of those mysteries that challenged the best scholars in searching Christian doctrine, and it has crowned the efforts of those who have discovered the truth. John had said chapter 1;v.14, "The Lord was made flesh and dwelt among us." (Look at the words of Paul in Philippians 2:5-8) To understand what is happening on Calvary, we must see Jesus as a human being. He was born in a natural way, although He was conceived in a supernatural way.

> He grew in stature and wisdom.
> He was subject to the laws of the land.
> He was tempted, and had the choice to yield, but He did not.
> He experienced thirst, hunger and pain.
> When His body was broken, He bled,
> When He was so severely stricken, He died.

All these happenings to Him are important in this word, "WHY?" from the lips of our Lord. This is the cry from a baffled human mind. It comes when all other answers have fled from His breaking heart.

Jesus had been forsaken before:
> Members of His family forsook Him.
> His hometown of Nazareth would not accept Him.
> The nation He came to save refused Him.

At His Cross the disciples had run away.

In every instance before, Jesus could always steal away into prayerful fellowship with His Father. In John 16:32 He told His disciples, "Behold, the hour cometh, yea is come, that ye shall be scattered every man to his own, and shall leave me. And yet, I am not alone, for the Father is with me."

Until now! In this hour, God the Father turns away from Him. He withdraws His sunlight, He withholds His counsel. He denies Jesus His presence! Why? It is because Jesus had voluntary emptied Himself of His heavenly glory, that He might come to earth to be man's Redeemer. In His humanity, He could not understand His Father's absence. All other religions have men seeking and reaching up to God. Christianity has God coming down to man.

II. THIS LEADS US TO THE GRACE OF GOD.

1. Just four days prior to the crucifixion when Jesus saw the shadows of the Cross closing in on Him, He cried to the Father. God came and spoke to Him words of comfort and assurance. Now at Calvary, Jesus hears only the echo of His own voice. What is the difference? The answer is found in that which is happening to Jesus on the Cross. The real clue is found in 2 Cor.5:21,"For God hath made Jesus to be sin for us, Who knew no sin, that we might be made the righteousness of God in Him." Remember? Isaiah had said, "He was wounded for our transgressions, He was bruised for our iniquities." Beloved, it was not the nails that held Him on that Cross, nor was it the Roman soldiers that kept Him there. Rather, it was His love for you and me that held Him in that place of death and destiny. Jesus became everything that we are, that by God's grace, we might become everything that He is. Hallelujah! What a Saviour!

**A Christian man was always going around praising God about everything he read. A son handed his dad a geography book. "Can you find anything in there to praise God about?" After a short while, "Well praise the Lord." WHY?" "It says here that the deepest ocean is over seven miles deep. Praise the Lord, that is where He has put my sins."

To show you some of the price Jesus paid for us on Calvary, name a sin. Any sin:

-Drunkenness, God made Jesus the representative of that ugly vice and crushed it by crushing Him.
-Fornication, (Same as above.)
-Pride,
-Murder,
-Homosexuality,
-Gossip. All are included.

Jesus overcame those vices that can overcome you. Whatever your sin is, or was, Jesus became that and was crushed to give you victory over it. Matthew Henry: "That one spot on Golgotha was the most hated place in all God's universe. And on it, God poured out His wrath against sin."

At Gethsemane Jesus had prayed, "Father, if it be possible, let this cup pass from me." He was not trying to back out of His destiny, He was not afraid of the pain. Rather, it was the fact, and act, of becoming sin, not sinful. By becoming sin, it meant He would be utterly separated from His Father. And that separation to Jesus was the agony of Hell. For Hell, in it's fullest sense means, God forsakened, God abandoned. Do you understand it? God had to forsake Christ, His only begotten Son, in order to forgive us, and to make us into His sons. Gal. 3:13: "Christ hath redeemed us from the curse of the law, being made a curse for us. For it is written, 'Cursed is everyone that hangeth on a tree.'" This means Jesus took the sinner's place and died the sinner's death. It means He took the full fury of God's anger against sin that separates man from Him.

**And anyone who thinks there is anything he can add to Calvary for his own salvation, simply does not understand what Jesus did for lost mankind on that fateful Cross the day when He died.

**There was an aged sick woman living in a Catholic community. Visited by the village priest. "Your sins are forgiven." "Let me see your hands." She examined them. "Sorry sir, but the One Who forgives me my sins has nail prints in His hands."

III. THROUGH JESUS CHRIST, GOD'S GRACE COVERED ALL OUR SIN WHEN WE TRUST HIM TO COVER IT WITH THE BLOOD OF THE LAMB

Calvary covers the law that condemns and uncovers the grace that forgives. Calvary covers our sin while it uncovers His salvation. God promises, "Him that cometh unto me I will in no wise cast out." John 6:37

CONCLUSION

As you sit in your house, you hear a sound. You search for the source, at your front door it is found. You open the door and there stands a man, that you've never met, with a check book in his hand. He says, "Go gather your bills and add them today, I have this check book. and I'd like to pay." You pause for a moment, this cannot be real! But you would be foolish to not take this deal. Now here's the surprise, this story is true. The door's not your house, It's inside of you. The 'debt' is your sin that you carry around, but Jesus will pay it, Now how does that sound? Yes, a check He will write with salvation's pen. There's a knock on your door, Will you let Him come in?   — Author unknown

"Your work on Monday can glorify the Lord as much as your worship on Sunday."

LABORERS TOGETHER WITH GOD

1 Corinthians 3:9-15

1. Elton Trueblood, in his book, <u>The Yoke of Christ,</u> makes an extraordinary statement about the common working place: "God may care more about factories and offices than about church buildings, because more people are in them more of the time." Let me give you something else to think about: It is impossible for any one to teach or preach anything of lasting value on Sunday at church, if they do not practice it themselves out in the work-a-day world on Monday. For, real faith works, and it works out there in the factory just as effectively as it works within the four walls of a church building!

2. Your work on Monday will testify to the depth of your worship on Sunday. Because many of you face hateful jobs in hostile public places, I want to give you some words of direction and encouragement.

**Here is an oldie: It seems that a clergyman and a bus driver arrived at the Pearly Gates at the same time. (You'll notice I did not say the preacher was a Baptist.) Anyway, the bus driver was first in the Awards line. He was given a golden halo and a Mercedes Benz to drive in Glory. The preacher stepped up with great expectations. "Look what that bus driver got. Man, I can't wait to see what they have for me to ride in." He was given a tin halo, a burlap robe and an old used skateboard. The preacher complained to St. Peter, "Now looka heah." (Southern) "I don't understand this at all. I was pastor of a large congregation back on earth. Men looked up to me, and respected me. That fellow ahead of me, he was only a bus driver." St. Peter: "Yep, you're right, only a bus driver. But the difference between you and him was in your work results. The way he drove the bus, he put people to praying. And the way you preached, you put people to sleep."

3. Now, the Lord did not make all people bus drivers and preachers. But He did equip most people to do certain work while on earth. And He expects every worker, administrator or bag boy to work in such a way as to serve others effectively through your work, and to glorify Him with your talent. "We are laborers together with God." That not only includes the ordained. It includes everybody. It includes you. "Every man's work shall be made manifest. "The Living Bible explains that verse this way, "There is going to come a time of testing at Judgment Day to see what kind of material each builder used." Do you see it? Your work on your job on Monday can glorify God as much as your worship on Sunday. Don't allow the world to define your work as either secular, or sacred. According to these verses in 1 Cor. 3, each person is accountable to God for services rendered.

4. God promotes work, and He is opposed to those who can work and won't work. 2 Thess.3:10, "If any man (will) not work, neither should he eat." That is God's method of thinning out lazy freeloaders on welfare rolls who are able to work, and choose not to work. And, before your compassion cancels out your reason, or vice versa, let me hasten to say absolutely, we should take care of those who cannot take care of themselves. The Bible is very clear and uncompromising in charging us to care for the widows and the fatherless, and the needy. But I am tired of hearing about men who come home to get their women pregnant, and then leave home until the welfare check is increased. Daddies are as much responsible for the upkeep of children as the mothers who birth them.

5. If you agree so far with what I have said, you can say "Amen." And if you   do, you'll get a bit of relief also.

**Elizabeth Barrett Browning wrote: "Free men freely work: Whoever fears God, fears to sit at ease. "I truly think when all believers appear before Christ's Judgment Seat for rewards in Glory, there will be a lot of faithful Christian secretaries, football players, farmers and carpenters who will be in line ahead of some of us preachers, simply because those "Laypeople" out-dedicated us in our work and in their work. This is not intended to put preaching down in any way, but it is a statement of fact that eternal rewards will not be based upon one profession being above another. It will be based upon our honesty and effort in fulfilling tasks we have been assigned. And a Christian fulfilling his role as a pharmacist, postman, sales person or security guard, is expected to be a living example and witness for Christ as much as a preacher standing behind any sacred pulpit. Elton Trueblood is probably correct. God could be as much concerned over the ordinary person on an ordinary job penetrating society every day, as He is in the preacher doing his duty in preaching God's truth. Preachers are called to preach the Gospel for people to hear it proclaimed. Saved people are to practice living the Gospel for the unsaved to see it in practice.

6. There is a Biblical revelation at the beginning of human existence that underscores our task on earth is to obey and serve God. And to do it well. Before the first man, Adam, awoke and discovered this wonderful and new world, God had already appointed work for him to do. To "have dominion over fish, foul, cattle and creeping things." Gen.1:12. And, the first words Adam heard was a challenge from the Lord, "Replenish the earth and subdue it."

**Any farmer or gardener can tell you that you don't subdue the earth and its green things by sitting under a tree and watching it grow.

7. Man was made to work! For two reasons: <u>Economic</u>: We must work to if we expect to eat. And <u>Therapeutic:</u> You must work to stretch your muscles and your mind. Eccle.5:12, "The sleep of a laboring man is sweet." Whether work is considered a blessing or a curse depends on the worker and his attitude towards his vocation.

** My Uncle Schaeffer White was a weaver in the Appleton mill in Anderson. He was also a preacher. One day he had to take off work to preach a funeral. He asked my daddy to work for him. Daddy did. Next day Daddy asked E.C. White, "That set of looms ran awful yesterday, how do you manage to run them so well?" Uncle: "Well, I ask the Lord to help me run them, and He does." And my dad answered, "Well, me and the devil didn't do such a good job running them yesterday." This question: Was the difference in the looms, or was the difference in the attitudes of the workers?

What about you and your job? Is it a dull routine, to be despised? If it is, I know someone who would gladly trade places with you, one who is unable to work. He sits confined to a wheel chair every day he is awake. He would love to run a machine, or sweep a floor, plow a mule or sell merchandise. Anything, if he could only walk.

8. There are some Bible admonitions concerning work and workmen. And when you apply them to your potential, they might give you strength to keep on at your vocation. John 5:17, "My Father worked hitherto, and I must work." Eccl. 9:10, "Whatsoever thy hand findeth to do, do it with thy might." Good work ethics brings honor to both laborer and the Lord. John 9:4, "Work, for the night cometh when no man can work." Time is limited. I Cor. 3:9, "We are laborers together with God." God won't call you to work where He cannot keep you. Col. 3:23, "And whatsoever you do, do it heartily, as to the Lord - and not unto men." This truth will bring worthiness to your workplace.

9. As a Christian, you can have confidence and courage to go to work each day if you will focus on two things: (a) that you are first, a servant of Jesus Christ, working for Him, working with Him. Because you are His child, you are representing Him in whatever you do. Someone has said, "I'd rather see a sermon any day than hear one." (b) The Gospel: if it is to be known by the unsaved, then it must be seen by them, when they see you, demonstrating the Gospel through your work. If you are a fast-food dishwasher, do it to the very best of your ability. If you are a shopkeeper, give 16 ounces to the pound., 12 inches to the foot, a dollar's work for a dollar's pay.

You may be the only one an unsaved person will see Jesus, as He works through you.

**Do you recall a man by the name of Paul Dietzel? Before he became Head Coach at the University of South Carolina, he was football coach at Louisana State University. And while he was at L.S.U., he was chosen "Coach of the Year," and his team was #1 in the nation. Coach Dietzel is one of those rare public persons who publicly puts God first in everything he does. He made this statement: "First came my own personal commitment to Christ as Lord and Saviour. Then came an evaluation of my life and habits. Obviously changes had to be made. Social drinking was one of those unnecessary and often negative practices that could go first of all. I decided to commit myself to church membership and activity. I also pledged to present my body as a living sacrifice to Jesus Christ. To seek His guidance through prayer; and to try to be myself, that's what I ask other young men to be." Concerning his livelihood, he further stated, "I realized that God is looking down on all these busy stadiums. Does He care about who wins in each one? I doubt it. But He does care about how His people live and act." Faith before football. I like that. There is nothing wrong with football, unless you leave God out of it. Nothing can have eternal value if the Lord is not in it.

10. God often comes to us for special reasons in our work.

**Can you just imagine Moses out there on the backside of the desert? He was there for a reason. He tried to stay away from people. He was a fugitive. God appeared to him in a burning bush. Moses saw the bush and walked over toward it. He heard a voice: "Moses, what are you doing out here on the backside of nowhere?" Moses: "Just minding my own business." If you will read the story in Exodus 3, using your sanctified imagination, you will discover that God gave Moses a mighty challenge at the burning bush. The Lord can take what we are and use it for our good and His glory. It does not take special people to do special things: "But I'm too old." God used an older Abraham. "But I'm too young." God used a young Timothy

"I'm not a good speaker." God chose Moses, a stutterer. "God can't use a sinner like me." God used David, a murderer and wife stealer.

> God used a streetwalker in Mary Magdalene.
> God used a short thief in Zacchaeus.
> God used a fearful Gideon to do a fearless job.

What am I saying? The only reason the Lord will not use you somewhere, no matter your talent, or lack of talent, is your unwillingness to let Him use you.

**I met an older black lady in the hospital. God was using her to hand out religious tracts. I had a neighbor whose mother was in her eighties who found a way to witness for her Lord. She would go into stores where they sell beer, and insert a Gospel tract in six-packs. Listen: anybody, anywhere, at any time can find a way to bear a witness for Jesus Christ. When Christ is their personal Lord and Saviour. You might want to pause and think seriously about that before you proceed further.

**One of the greatest preachers 3 or 4 generations ago was Dr. George Truett, pastor of First Baptist Church in Dallas, Texas. He once got discouraged and he wanted to quit preaching. He had a close friend in Police Chief Arnold. They went quail hunting together. Dr. Truett's gun accidentally discharged, killing Chief Arnold. All Dallas was shocked. Dr. Truett was so grieved, he shut himself off from the public and decided he would never preach again. But on Saturday night he finally fell asleep for the first time since the accident. He dreamed that Jesus came to his bedroom. Jesus stood by his side and spoke to him, "Be not afraid. You are My Man from now on." He awoke and told his wife about the dream. He fell asleep again, and again the same dream. It happened a third time. And the following Sunday morning, Dr. Truett returned to his pulpit and preached for many more years. It was because God appeared to him and promised him that He would be with him in the work the Lord had called him to do. When you know God is with you, you can face anything and do anything. God appeared unto Moses in a burning bush. He appeared to Dr. Truett in a dream. And the Lord appears to you now in His Word and in this promise, "I will be with thee, even unto the end of the age."

11. Remember those shepherds of Bethlehem? 1200 years after Moses. They were out there doing a very menial task. Shepherding sheep like Moses, working. And God sent to them a sky full of angels. They went to see the Christ Child. They returned to their sheep. But I believe they were never the same after that night of angels and adoration of Christ. They were simple men, doing their job to make a living. And God turned their routine into a renewal! And if you are observant, He will do the same for you in your work. The Lord can touch a hurting world through your daily work, and He will use you to make contact with people who are out of contact with Him. Hey! Turn that blue Monday into a blessed Monday. Use it as an opportunity to lend a helping hand, to share a little Christian love and light to other folks around you.

**George Washington Carver was born a slave. Yet he used what God gave him to discover so many by-products of the lowly peanut. Do you enjoy peanut butter? Carver was the inventor. This man wrote a bulletin to farmers: "105 ways of preparing the peanut for human consumption." He is credited with the creation of 300 products from the peanut and 150 products from the sweet potato. He appeared before the Senate Agriculture Committee in Washington, D.C. One Senator asked, "Mr. Carver, where did learn so much about the peanut?" Carver: "I learned it from the Bible." Senator: "But what does the Bible teach about peanuts?" Carver: "The Bible teaches nothing about the peanut. But it told me about God, and God told me about the peanut." Case closed! All was from the Lord Who directed his abilities and revealed to him the methods by which he should work. Cooperation with the Lord in your work will bring honor to God through your work.

12. And beloved, have you thought about it. Your work may be in a dark corner somewhere. God knows that. He has put you there to be a light for somebody's darkness.

**Years ago there was a devout Catholic Monk who was called Brother Lawrence. He was an inspiration to everybody around him. He was asked why he was always so cheerful. He said when he was baking bread, and sweeping the floor in the monastery kitchen, that he had a great a sense of Christ's presence as when he was kneeling in the chapel.

13. Dear Brothers and Sisters, the whole indoor and outdoor world can be a sacred place when you take Jesus with you, wherever you walk and wherever you work - That's Christian witnessing at its best. That kind of living puts purpose above paycheck.

<u>CONCLUSION</u>

There was once a doctor called to a church where the pastor had collapsed. A huge snowstorm was blowing. The doctor knew the pastor needed immediate surgery. But the snow prevented them from taking the pastor to the hospital. The doctor looked around, and spotted the huge table at the altar. He had some of the parishioners to clean it off. They placed the pastor on the altar. The operation began and was completed an hour or so later. The doctor-surgeon was wiping perspiration from his brow, and he saw these words imbedded on the altar: "Glory to God in the Highest." The physician said he was overwhelmed with a new sense of appreciation, that through his work he could experience and share the glory of God.

You, too, can find ways to glorify the Lord in your work, when you remember, "We are laborers together with God." Amen.

"Angels were created to be God's agents,
attendants and messengers"

ANGELS - AGENTS OF GOD

Psalm 91:1-12

Read Psalm 91:1-12. Note especially verses 11-12. John Calvin: "Angels are the dispensers and administrators of Divine beneficence toward us. They regard our safety, undertake our defense, direct our ways, and exercise a constant solicitude that no evil befall us."

** One of our SBC ministers had a daughter to go away to college. In that college town a wierdo was attacking and assaulting young women. One evening she was leaving the library. As she walked toward her car, she saw a man standing beside a tree. When she saw his face, fear gripped her heart. She prayed for God's protection. Nothing happened. She got in to her car and drove away. That same evening another coed walked the same path. She was attacked and assaulted. The man was apprehended. The preacher's daughter agreed to testify against the man. On the stand the culprit was asked, "Why did you not attack the first young lady?" He said, "Well, there was this great big football-type guy walking with her..." And the girl thought she was alone...(I have several versions of this story)

Beloved, angels are mentioned being on the earth in the first book of the Bible and also in the last book of the Bible. They were present at creation and they will be here at the Consummation. They will also be in attendance at the Coronation. So, let's look deeper into this matter of God's unseen helpers.

I. WHO ARE THE ANGELS, AND HOW DO WE KNOW THEY EXIST?

1. First of all, we go to the source of authority — God's Holy Word. Yes, angels did exist before the creation of the earth. In Job 38:4-

7, the Lord is speaking to Job, "Where were you when I laid the foundation of the earth? Tell me, if you understand, on what were its footings set, or who laid the cornerstone while the morning stars sang together and <u>the angels</u> shouted for joy?" The KJV says "sons of God." The reference is to ethereal, supernal beings. In the O.T. there at least 100 references to these creations of God. 150 references in the N.T.

**Billy Graham has written: "I am convinced that these heavenly beings exist, and that they provide unseen aid on our behalf. I do not believe in angels because someone has told me about a dramatic visitation from an angel. I do not believe in angels because UFOs are angel-like in some of their reported appearances. I do not believe in angels because ESP experts are making the realm of the spiritual world seem more and more plausible. I do not believe in angels because of the sudden worldwide emphasis on the reality of Satan and demons. I do not believe in angels because I have ever seen one. I do believe in angels because the Bible states there are angels, and I believe the Bible to be the true Word of God."

2. After the creation, and after Adam and Eve's fall, we see the cherubims placed with flaming swords at the gate of Eden's Garden. (Gen.3:24) In Ezekiel, chapters 1 and 10, we find them as guardians of Paradise and special attendants to God. Angels became visualized when they appeared to Abraham, telling him that Sarah was to become a mother in her advanced age. Two angels from the Lord warned Lot the wicked cities of Sodom and Gomorrah were under God's judgment, and soon would be destroyed. It was an angel that led Abraham's servant to find a wife for Isaac. It was an angel that left the signature of God on Jacob's thigh in the wilderness. An angel invaded a lion's den at God's command. He protected Daniel by locking the jaws of the lions with invisible glue that shook Darius in his kingly boots. Moses met an angel at the burning bush.

And in the New Testament, in that night of all nights, when Jesus was born, shepherds huddled with their flocks near Bethlehem - (Read about it in Luke 2:8-14). We do not have to wait until December to be blessed anew with the greatest of all announcements. ANGELS were in attendance at the birth of our Lord. ANGELS were near him throughout His ministry. ANGELS were with Christ when He ascended to Heaven, and ANGELS will be with Him when He returns: "When the Son of man shall come in all His glory, and all the holy angels with Him." Matt.25:31. When the Apostle Peter was thrown in jail for preaching Jesus, an angel came in the night. Waking Peter up and told him to get ready to leave the jail. Peter obeyed, and the angel opened the locked doors...and guess what, Peter went right back onto the streets and started preaching God's Word again.

3. Angels, Cherubim, Seraphim: What are they?

a. Angels are <u>created beings</u>: Col.1:16 says, "For by Christ were all things created that are in Heaven, in earth, visible and invisible." They were created to be God's agents, attendants and messengers. Also, to minister to God's saints on earth. "Are they not all ministering spirits, sent forth to minister for them who shall be heirs of salvation?" Hebrews 1:14. "Ministering spirits" is speaking of angels. "Heirs of salvation" is speaking of believers, people who trust God as Sovereign. Christ as our Saviour, and the Holy Spirit as our Sustainer.

b. Angels <u>are spirits</u> - they can travel as fast as thought. they can pass through material objects. Angels are sexless - they do not procreate. And although they are spirits, they are not to be worshipped.

c. How else do we know angels exist, other than the Bible? Because of human experience and exchanges with them. Call me whatever, but I have glimpsed them near me. I have actually seen their forms.

**Corrie Ten Boom told about being taken to a German prison. All Jews were ordered to strip and put on prison garments. Corrie prayed the Germans would not see her Bible she had wrapped in some clothing. She told of going through the search line. The lady in front of her was searched. Corrie passed by unsearched, as if the guards did not ever see her. The lady behind her was searched, as well as the whole group of prisoners, EVERYONE EXCEPT CORRIE! She believes God sent an angel to blind the eyes of the guards, causing them to overlook her and the Bible. And that Bible proved to be a special strength to her and other prisoners for months and months.

**When I was in the Navy during World War II, I spent several days in New Hebrides. At that time I did not know about Missionary John G. Patton, nor did I know the local natives were once savages. Patton had heard of many white people being killed by cannibals in New Hebrides. He prayed that the Lord would let him go to take the Gospel to these people. His family tried to dissuade him. But he went anyway. One night he awoke to the sounds of restless natives. He looked outside to see a band of cannibals who had come to burn down his house and kill him. They stood near the house most of the night. But nothing happened. Weeks later, Patton was in the area from which that particular group of killers had come to his house. The chief had recently become a Christian. So, Patton asked him, "Aren't you the one who came with your warriors to burn my house that night?" The chief told him it was true. "That's why we came. But we stopped when we saw those soldiers with shields and swords standing outside your house. Where did they come from?" Patton told the chief he and his wife were in the house, alone. You and I know where they came from. They were sent from Heaven to protect God's servants.

**Review 2 Kings 2, with Elisha and the young man at Dothan.

II. ARE ANGELS ACTIVE TODAY? Yes, they are!

1. They are present to give assurance and protection to God's people.

** My brother Lee, says he believes he has encountered his guardian angel twice. Once when he was drinking and gambling. He and several others were in the woods playing poker for money. The other men became angry with him. He felt threatened. Suddenly a man walked up to the group. Lee introduced himself. And this person said, "Yes, I know who you are." Lee told me the man was a perfect stranger to him. This encounter settled the dispute and probably saved Lee from physical harm. Another time Lee was going to get on a ride at the county fair. This same man came up and said, "I'll ride with you." They boarded the ride. And it suddenly stopped running. It broke down. Lee feels this was protection from a disaster that was about to happen. He never saw the man again. In his own words he told me he believes this person was his guardian angel. Sometimes you can feel someone holding you back when you want to rush headlong into some project or position. At other times you can feel them pushing you ahead when you feel uncertain about moving forward.

  **I have had people to tell me, "You know, I don't come to church often, but something made me come today. And I am glad I did. Your message was meant for me." Angel nudging is what I call it. Be sure to obey these holy impulses.

**A good many years ago my brothers and sisters celebrated the fiftieth Golden Wedding Anniversary of my parents in Anderson. I was pastor at Woodfields Baptist Church in Greenwood, SC. We lived about 40 minutes away from the anniversary site. My wife and I hurried towards Anderson after Morning Worship. Suddenly my wife screamed. A pickup truck came out of a side road to my left, failing to heed the stop sign. He was traveling so fast, I did not see him until he had passed onto the right side of my automobile. One second made the difference between a horrible crash and our safety. I believe an angel either held us back that one second, or nudged him ahead one second. Otherwise, the potential crash could have caused the death of five people. I'll always believe an angel directed my driving that day. Saving us for further ministry in God's Kingdom work.

III. ANOTHER SET OF QUESTIONS

How many angels are there? Do they have names?

1. How many angels? The warriors at New Hebrides saw a band of them surrounding Patton's home. There were ten thousand with Moses on Mt. Sinai. In Psalms 68:17 it speaks of "The chariots of God are 20,000, even thousands of angels." Heb. 12:22, "But ye have come unto Mt. Zion, and unto the city of the living God, the heavenly Jerusalem - and to an innumerable (unnumbered) company of angels." And in Rev. 5 there is recorded an angelic choir that praises the Lamb. "Ten thousand times ten thousand and thousands of thousands." I'd say that has to be a great crowd of these supernal creatures. Legions of them.

2. And their names?   One is Michael
                      Another is Gabriel.
                      Then there is Lucifer. Is. 14:12

CONCLUSION

An excellent story about an angel was reported in Reader's Digest some years ago. Dr. S.W. Mitchell was a celebrated Philadelphia neurologist. One wintry night he was awakened by a knock on the door of his home. Dr. Mitchell opened the door to find a little girl, poorly dressed, and deeply upset. She told the doctor her mother was very ill, and she desperately needed a doctor. She asked if he would go and see her. It was a bitterly cold night, but Dr. Mitchell dressed and went with the child. He found the mother ill with pneumonia. After tending to her immediate needs, he made arrangements for additional care. As the doctor prepared to leave, he complimented the woman for having such a brave and intelligent daughter. The woman looked at him strangely, and said, "But my daughter died a month ago. Her shoes and coat are in the closet over there." Dr. Mitchell was so astonished that he went to the closet and opened the door. There was the coat the child had worn when she came to his house that night. He felt the coat. It was dry and warm. Dr. Mitchell told the story after he was convinced that God allowed an angel, in the form of her child, to come to him from the "other world" on behalf of a dying mother.

Does it not thrill you, a believer, to know you never have to be alone? When Lazarus died, he "was carried by the angels into Abraham's bosom." Luke 16:22. The angels are your friends because they are the agents of God.   Amen.

"David finds himself in a hateful place among hostile people."

AMONG THE LIONS

Psalm 57:1-4

It is not always easy to live the Christian life in an unchristian environment. Snakes and skunks, doves and sheep cannot live together in perfect peace and harmony.

1. Turn in your Bibles to Psalm 57 and I'll show you what I mean. Read verses 1, 2, 3, as follows:

V. 1   David's Recourse — A positive choice he has made.
        "My soul trusteth in Thee." His life anchor. A Pilot in the darkest night. A Friend on the brightest day.

V. 2   His Resource — A constant supply.
        "Unto God that performeth all things for me."
        At the spout where the glory comes out.

V. 3   David's Refuge — Confirmation for his trust.
        "God shall send forth His mercy and His truth."
        His healings, hope and help.

I don't know about you, but there have been times when my valley seemed so low and so long, I needed a light tap on the shoulder from the Lord to remind me that He was with me. My wife of 56 years had died. The next day I went to her grave and talked a while with her. When I was ready to leave, I told her, "Geraldine, if you can hear me, I just want to say again how much I love you." I was holding on to the tent pole at her graveside. Suddenly it started quivering. A gust of wind came down just as I spoke those words, "If you can hear me." The wind lasted little more than five seconds. I was thrilled. I looked heavenward and said, "Thank you, Lord." I knew He was there. Perhaps my wife was there also. And I think

109

this kind of expectation is Biblical: James 4:8, "Draw nigh to God and He will draw nigh to thee." God will give direction to us in our earthly pilgrimage. And He is ever ready to give His strength for our weaknesses. See 2 Cor. 12:9. Verse 4 shows why David is crying out to God: "My soul is among the lions." <u>WHAT</u>? David is not like Daniel in the lions' den. David finds himself in a hateful place among hostile people. David, a child of God, is being abused by the enemies of God.Thoughtless people, careless tongues, spiteful creatures. A holy man exposed to unholy surroundings. This happening is spelled out in Lam. 3:46 "All our enemies have opened their mouths against us." Accusing. Lying. Threatening. Swearing.

** Our military people are among the lions in Iraq. Many Arabs and Muslims hate us, and are sworn to kill us. There are some rich Arabs who will pay families for suicide bombers to kill Americans. Our troops die to free Arabs who don't know enough about freedom to desire it. Terrorists are lions who hide in protective holy sites. Arab lions blew up flights 93 and 175. They blasted a large hole in the hulk of the U.S.S. Cole. They blew up embassies, beheaded some of our allies, while thousands celebrated these barbaric executions in the streets. Our President, in his own heart of peace, really believes we can restructure a warring people who have lived like violent, kill or be killed, lions for more than 2,000 years. "There is no fear of Jehovah before their eyes." Ps. 36:1

2. I know most of you can identify with David's outcry through circumstances in your own daily lives at work, in school, or maybe in your own home. How do you feel when a dirty mouth uses the heavenly Father's name in vain. Swearing? How do you react to vulgar stories that are told by vulgar people? Are you ever tempted to follow the crowd that follows not God?

And while you are among the saints, are you saintly? And when you are among the lions, do you roar like them?

Jesus certainly knew who were His lambs and who were the lions. To the church-belonging lions He said, "Ye hypocrites...you draw nigh unto me with your lips. But your heart is far from God." Matt. 15:7-8

**It saddened me to learn one of my deacons had a foul mouth in his workplace. He prayed in church like a deacon ought to pray. He died in his sleep one night. And I have a feeling he was also sad when He faced God as his Judge.

LISTEN! It is OK to be out with the in-crowd, when the in-crowd is out with God. Anyone who lies down with dogs is sure to get fleas. (Anybody here feel itchy?)

3. Look, I know where I'm coming from. I was once a sailor. And before I became a Christian, I could cuss as bad as the baddest. My common speech was vulgar, insulting! However! When the Lord of miracles changed this lion into a lamb,

> —My profanity turned to praise.
> —My lustful appetite changed to appropriate desires.
> —My direction changed.
> —My destiny changed.

Now I ask you, why would I want to turn from the Saviour back to the sewer? Why would any child of God want to turn back to walk with a Godless people.

**When I entered the U.S. Navy I was 17 years old. All the recruits slept in a gym-like building the first night. That night a young man near me took out a Bible and read it silently. He then knelt by his bedside and prayed. Well! When us "lions" saw that. We laughed at him. Mocked him. Someone asked, "Are you your mama's baby?" Let me tell you, three months later when we entered our first combat, knowing we could be blasted into eternity with one bomb, Those of us who mocked, we cried out to the Shepherd of the lambs to spare us, poor humbled lions.

Now let me give you lambs some advice about "Facing the Lions."

I. YOU DON'T TAME LIONS BY IMITATING THEM

.

**Some years ago several of my family members visited my brother out in Houston, Texas. On our way home we stopped by New Orleans to visit Audubon Park, a wonderful zoo. I was walking up ahead of my wife, sister and brother-in-law. There was an outside, single pen with a large chimpanzee sitting on a shelf. The front of the pen was covered with wire. Some young boys were teasing the chimp. They would go to a fountain, get some water in their mouths, and go back to spit it on the chimp. The chimpanzee, in turn, would climb down from its perch, get a mouthful of water from its bowl, and return to the shelf. When the next person came close to the pen, he would spit the water on them. I couldn't wait for my brother-in-law, Bennie, to walk up to the pen. He got water spewed all over him. The chimp was aping the children. (Pardon the pun) But you never, ever tease a lion that way. Listen and learn. The lions are left to the lion-tamer and his expertise. And the human lions must be left to the Divine Lion-Tamer. You must learn to leave certain bothersome people to the Lord. People who irritate you, accuse you, and despise you.

**I had to do that to a beer joint owner when she tried to chastise me for entering her place and calling out 3 church members who were there drinking her beer. I could have scolded her for selling beer, but I left her to the Lord's care.

II. AND YOU NEVER HAVE TO FIGHT ALONE WHEN YOU ARE AMONG THE SNARLING, BITING LIONS

Jesus told His disciples just before He ascended to glory, "Lo, I am with thee, even unto the end." Matt. 28:20

Lo, I am with thee — in church.
Lo, I am with thee — in school.
Lo, I am with thee — on the job.
Lo, I am with thee — even among the lions.

1. And when you walk through the dark valley of persecution, although you are wounded by cruel lions, never forget you don't

have to face the lions alone. And though you are wounded in some way by the lions, the Lord will heal. David later said, "He anointeth my head with oil." Especially healing oil.

The third thing:

III. YOU CAN SAY "NO" TO THE LIONS

"No" can become one of the biggest words in your vocabulary - Since you are one of God's lambs "Would you like to hear a juicy story?" "No, thanks"

EMPOWERMENT COMES WHEN YOU — —-

— Say NO to flirtations and sex outside of marriage.
— Say NO to cheating in school.
— Say NO to popping pills at parties.
— Say NO to political parties that endorse immorality.
— Say NO to beer guzzling and booze parties.
— Say NO to Sunday trips to the mountains and beaches.
— Say NO to anything that would cause a complete stranger to think you might be a lion instead of God's lamb.

IV. DO PRAY FOR BROTHERS WHO WORK AMONG THE LIONS

**Our military men and women are among lions in Iraq. Pray for them. Sometimes they cannot tell who will try to kill them next. They live daily among radical insurgents who hate them. Pray for these lambs among the lions.

1. As a Christian, you have access to a hot line to Heaven. By your intercession you can help lift the burden of a fellow believer. It is possible for YOU to be God's answer to their prayer!

**Back in depression days a church had met to pray for a needy family. While they were praying, a child came into the church with a wagon filled with potatoes and beans. He told the congregation, "Pa said he didn't have time to join you, but he sent his prayers."

2. Our Lord knows how to make ice without an icemaker. He knows how to make a feast from a fistful of food.

3. The Lord knows how to deliver a blanket in response to prayer.

**A medical missionary was deep in the heart of Africa claiming souls for Christ as he cooperated with God in mending sick people. An emaciated pregnant woman was brought to his primitive compound. The baby was born, but the mother died. There were no blankets nor adequate clothing for the baby. The doctor asked two nurse assistants to lie down and keep the baby warm between them. Later that afternoon the missionary was teaching some children. He told about the baby and its need for a blanket. In prayer he asked the children to pray for the child to live through the night. And one of the children prayed, "And please send this baby a blanket — and a little dolly for my sick friend." Next day the baby was still living. That afternoon a box filled with clothing and other things arrived from America. The missionary had the children to help in opening the box. It contained toothbrushes and paste, pictures and writing materials. It also had some cookies and canned goods. The little girl who prayed for a blanket spotted one in the bottom of the box. Everyone was exhilarated. Under the blanket was a small doll! The box had been prepared at a church several weeks earlier. They had no knowledge of the need for a blanket. They didn't know, but God did! And it was done. Baby doll and all.

4. The Lord is not blind that He cannot see the needs of His sheep. He is not deaf to the pleas of His flock. Nor is He ignorant of His lambs who work out among the lions. Jesus was once a Shepherd here on earth, and He is the Great Shepherd watching over His sheep from Heaven this day, and every day!

5. David, the shepherd boy, once faced a real lion. 1 Sam. 17:34-35 (Read to congregation.) And in that same chapter he is ready to face

a 9-ft. giant who is the enemy of Israel. In Psalm 57 David is a bit fearful and frustrated by some people who presented him and threatened him. David is saying, "It is like being among lions that want to kill and devour you." Christian, what are you to do when you find yourself near the public lions that want to challenge you, to corrupt you, and to change your faith?

CONCLUSION

OK, let me sum it up for you.

1. <u>Do not conform to the crowd:</u> Rom. 12:1,"Be not conformed to this world (of lions), but be ye transformed by the renewing of your mind - that you may prove (to the lions) what is that good, and acceptable, and perfect will of God (is)" Live that your life will be attractive and different.

2. <u>Do not compromise:</u> Some church people will give a little here and there, just to get along.

**I think it was Aesop who told about the fox offering the robin a worm for one of its feathers. He did this daily until the robin lost so many feathers he no longer was able to fly. Then the fox ate him. Satan knows your weakness and he knows how to rob you of peace.

It is possible some people have compromised their testimony away. And now they stand before a world with no effective witness for the Lord.

LISTEN! It is better to be accused of being "holier than thou" than to hear it echoing in the soul, "You're drifting too far from the shore."

**I stood beside the deathbed of a bright and gifted man who had compromised his faith in God. And now he was about to die. He repented, and he told me to "Go back to the church and tell the people not to drift too far from the Lord, before it is too late." I did. And now I'm telling you.

3. Although I have done it before, don't shake your finger at them and tell them by tongue and body language, that God has reserved the hottest places in hell for them.

Many of you know what I have been talking about today:

— A Christian child who loves God's church, but has un-Christian, non-cooperating parents.
— A Christian husband living with an un-Christian wife.
— A Christian wife who lives with an ungodly husband. He demands Sunday dinner at noon, therefore keeping the wife from worship.

These wounded sheep don't need your scorn and criticism. They need your encouragement and prayers.

If you're one of God's suffering lambs, don't give up nor give out. Every Lord's Day, and other days, there are some of us who understand and pray for you who are in some bitter predicaments at home, at work, or at school. We want to share your burden and somewhat help to ease your load. And your personal fellowship with other lambs of God on Sunday makes it a bit easier for you to face the lions on Monday.

**And with this story I close this message. In the book, <u>Pilgrim's Progress,</u> the main character is Christian. It is the story of one man' journey on his way to the Celestial City of God. In one chapter Christian is accompanied by Timorous and Fearful(?). As they walk along together, they look up ahead and see lions lying by the roadside. When Timorous and Fearful see this threat, they turn and run back from whence they came. But Christian (Pilgrim) went forward. He too, felt a sense of fear. But as he neared them, he saw something else. He saw the lions were chained. He passed them by and went on to enter the City.

Dear lamb of God,

    The Lord knows who you are.

    The Lord knows where you are.

    And He knows where you are headed.

    And praise the Lord, He knows how to chain lions near you.

    And this very morning every person here is walking toward your destiny. You are either walking with the Lord towards Glory, or you are walking alone towards defeat, despair and doom.

Choose this day with whom you will walk through life and on into eternity. Amen

"They tied His holy and helping hands."

LIMITING GOD

Psalm 78:25-41

There is a fascinating verse of Scripture found in Psalm 78.41. It addresses a fundamental problem for believers. "Yea, they (Israel) turned their back and tempted God, and limited the Holy One of Israel."

WHAT? God - Who is the Creator behind all creation.
          God - Who is the Lawmaker of all good laws
          God - Who is the Designer behind all that is beautiful in this world...
          Does He have limitations?

WHY, Everybody knows that God is all-wise, Omniscient.
          That God is everywhere, Omnipresent.
          That God is Omnipotent, all powerful.

In Job 26:7-14, "(God) stretched out the north over the empty space and hung the earth upon nothing. He sets the boundary for the oceans, and a boundary for the day and night. By His power the seas grow calm, and the heavens are made beautiful through His Spirit. These are some of the minor things He does. Merely a whisper of His power."

Our God had but to speak for the planets and stars to come forth to spangle the universe in glittering splendor. Just a wave of His creative hand and life energized the unseen atom. God and Christ have fashioned the whole world, all therein and there out. From the microscopic to the astronomic, and each part of His creation celebrates the greatness of His glory for those who have ears to hear, eyes to behold, and hearts to believe.

BUT! There are some things God can't do and won't do until we work in cooperation with Him. (I made that statement at the beginning of a revival.) And one of the members came out the door furious, and told me, "My God can do anything!" She must have turned off her listening device after I told the congregation it is possible for us to restrict and limit the Lord. Surely she did not hear me out. The Lord has stored the hills with hardened stone; yet He has not chosen to create a single cathedral of glass, nor a pipe organ, nor a lovely chandelier. This does not mean He can't do it. But He hasn't yet. This means He will do certain things only with our cooperation. He fills the earth with iron ore. However, He has not elected to create a sewer's needle, nor a locomotive from deposits of iron ore. He gives life into every leaf and to everything that grows, the giant oak, the tall pine. Yet He has not created a log cabin nor a stately building.

And I believe the Lord wants me to remind you of something else, and it comes out of Ps.78:41. "Israel turned their back upon God and limited the Holy one of Israel." Now imprint this in your memory. The Lord God had intended to do much more for Israel. But those disobedient people refused to hear and obey His Voice. And they deliberately turned their backs and their wills upon the Lord. By doing this, they tied His holy and helping hands. They limited Him. They restricted Him. Remember Matt. 13:58, when Jesus was in Nazareth, "He did not many mighty works there_ because of their unbelief_." Could He do them? Of course He could. Did He do them? No! Because of their human doubt. Do you see it? Mighty works of God are possible and available, but the people would not allow themselves to become holy vessels through whom Jesus could do His mighty works.

This is the same thing that happened to Israel. By their disobedience and backsliding, they stopped the flow of God's blessings from Heaven to and through their nation. They limited Him by their disobedience.

I must tell you that some Christians have stopped the flow of God's intended blessings by their own stubbornness and unbelief. The main reason is they have gone off the deep end of their spiritual freedom. They think they can believe anything they choose to believe. Attend church when they feel like it, or stay away when they feel like it. Giving God the leftovers after they pay for their luxuries. Go where it is a shame for Christians to go, and still believe they have it made with God. They have approached the spiritual covenant this way. "God, You give up some of Your holiness and we'll give up a bit of our sinfulness. And then we can get together." That is a lie suggested by the devil. Let me tell you something. In your sins, big and small, you can no more reach God in His holiness, than a pig can fly on its own to the moon.

And this is getting us to my main message today.

Most Protestant churches plan annual revivals or some form of renewal. Yet, the question remains, can we have a church revival? Can we have a church revitalized? Let me rush to tell you, the Lord of Glory will not give a life-cleansing, soul-saving, devil defeating, Holy Spirit anointed revival to an un-willing church.

   —I have seen deacons who wanted their pastor to have revival.
   —I have seen preachers who wanted the deacons revived.

But I have seen only a few church members who are willing to pay the personal price for God's kind of revival. I can tell you one thing for sure. Either it is going to be revival in our nation, or there is going to be ruin.

| **Wm. Vaught: | "The handwriting on the wall of five continents now tells us that the day of judgment is at hand." |
| ** Prof. Albert Webber: | "To one endowed with a historical perspective, it must be clear that we are at the end of history as we know it." |

**Arnold Toynbee: "The stable characteristics of the past 6,000 yearsof civilized history are being changed and are falling apart."

These are not the ranting and ravings of incompetent alarmists. Rather, they are the sane judgments of men who have looked into the failures of past generations and they see the same seeds of failure being sown in our own time.

** Billy Graham has said, "Wherever evil is sown, the seed of judgment is sown at the same time.

** Ruth Graham,   in researching materials for a book has said, "Either God is going to punish America for her sins, or He will have to apologize to Sodom and Gomorrah."

Vance Havner sounded this clarion call in our denomination for more than 60 years. I heard him speaking at a pastors' retreat a good many years ago: He told us he saw three possibilities ahead:

1. The return of our Lord. His coming is a certainty. His soon coming is a possibility. Never have the prophetic signs been lined up together, as they are now.

2. He said believers could be overrun and overcome by unbelievers, as did the Roman Empire in the First Century. And, if this happens, the church would have to go underground. Or,

3. There could come a spiritual awakening all over America. We now live in a day of great potential, and at the same time, a day of great peril.

BUT GOD HAS A SOLUTION! 2 Chronicles 7:14 still holds, "If my people which are called by my name, shall humble themselves, and pray and seek my face; then will I hear (them) from Heaven, and I will forgive their sins, and heal their land." I tell you, I am deeply concerned about that verse, its promise and its potential. Also the peril we face if we claim not the promise. God, in this verse the Lord is addressing His own people, and He is reminding us of the same thing today. This is God's formula for revival: When we do four things, He will do three.

(1) <u>Humble Ourselves</u> Humility is a forgotten virtue among many believers that I know and some you may know. How many of us strut into church on a Sunday morning, or evening, as if we are doing God a great favor by showing up? Repentant tears are seldom seen in our churches anymore.

(2) <u>Pray:</u> Real prayer locks us in gear with the power that moves this universe! How long has it been since you were bowed in surrender at the feet of Jesus? Confessing your sin and asking for His special cleansing? Confessing your emptiness and asking for His glorious filling? Hear this promise in Jere. 29:13, "Ye shall seek me and find me, when ye shall seek for me with all your heart." If you find your-self shackled, bound and enslaved by one of Satan's sins, "Call and I will hear you.... And "if the Son shall set you free, ye shall be free indeed!" Hell has never forged a chain that Heaven cannot break. Pray people, and keep on praying.

(3) We are told to "<u>Seek God's face</u>." It's more like we seek God's favor. Often we chart our own course and ask God to endorse our choices. Many times we will pray to get our circumstances changed while God wants to change our character.

(4) "<u>Turn from your wicked ways</u>." Anything is wicked if it keeps you away from God and His church. How many church members spend God's tithes for earth's treasure? That is wicked. Some church members think they are superior in some way and have a right to criticize the brethren. Gossiping! I want to tell you, God is taping all the time.

**One Baptist went to Florida for a vacation and came back with a sun burned tongue. Know what I'm talking about?

Here is a shocker for you: You can find fellowship in a beer joint or lounge that is closer to what God wants for his church. They accept one another, warts, weaknesses and whatever.

Wouldn't it be glorious on a Sunday morning if all members of the church showed up, cleaned up, and prayed up? And we could all worship together in one accord, in the beauty of the Lord? Christians must have a holy purpose in worship if they want to have spiritual power and get some needed spiritual results.

As believers, we can do some things by working hard and planning well. We can then expect to get what man can do. However, when we plug in to God's purpose and power, we'll get what God can do. I'll guarantee you one thing, if we have a real revival, some folks are going to get upset, and everybody will get on fire. Either fiery glad or fiery mad. Yet, there are some folk so married to their pet sins, they are unready and unwilling to give them up for Jesus. What a pity. What a shame. What a loss.

Remember how the Apostle Paul would go into a town and stir the people up for God? They ran him out of several towns. And, do you know who hated him most? The religious people, the self-righteous people and people who are unwilling to do it God's way. People locked in to fruitless traditions.

**I wish I could have had a personal discussion with the lady who said her God could do anything. I would have enjoyed asking her:
>Can God give revival to a self-righteous church member?
>Can God give peace to a disobedient child?
>Can God give salvation to an unrepentant sinner?
>Can God take an unsaved person to Heaven?

That lady did not come back to the revival meeting because she was locked in to her own closed mind, and I believe she "Limited the Holy One of Israel" for herself.

LISTEN: Our God is not going to force anyone to be revived.
God is not going to take anyone to Heaven against their will.
But the dear Lord is ready and willing to give revival: How?

1. When we are ready and willing to put the Lord first at the center of our church, at the center of our secular activities. In any church program, whether it is the Choir, Women's work, Brotherhood, or Sunday School, if God and His purpose are not the heart of that program, we need to give it a burial; or by proper dedication, we can give it a resurrection.

2. I'm afraid some churches have lost their purpose for existence. A church can deteriorate into a community club, coming together for good times of fun and fellowship. I believe in fun and fellowship in a local church; but I believe these should be by-products of a higher and holier reason for our meeting together in Jesus' name.

It is my conviction that Christians should meet (a) To do some house cleaning and personal confession of sins. Offering and asking forgiveness where there has been personal conflict. (b) To fellowship in real communion with the Lord.

3. To get our eyes focused on God and His goals for us personally, and for our church.

4. To get empowered to go out to reach the un-reached for the Lord.

**I sat on a porch one day in Horse Creek Valley talking with a brilliant young man about faith in the Lord Jesus Christ. But his intellect had been captivated by Satan. His role models were agnostic Bob Ingersoll, atheist and Communist Lenin. He sat there discussing man's inhumanity to man. He talked about a great society based on the teachings of Karl Marx. I told him this is impossible. That man, at his best, was destroying himself and his world. That with wisdom of all the ages, men used their wisdom to build walls to keep people out, and constructed bombs to get rid of any threat to their lifestyle and their lust. I told him that man's only hope is to found in Jesus Christ, the Prince of Peace. He told me, " I can't accept that." So I quoted John 3:36 "He that believeth on the Son hath everlasting life, and he who believeth not the Son shall not see life, but the wrath of God abideth on him." He told me, "If that verse is true, then I am damned." I walked away from that young man with tears in my soul.

But here is my confession. There have been times when my own heart has been so cold, that I would not have gone out of my way to tell that young man that I loved him and God loved him. Beloved, we need revival when the trumpet in the pulpit makes an uncertain sound. We need revival when church members remain dry-eyed in a hell-bound world.

**Bob Ingersol, the bold agnostic of another generation, wrote on the fly leaf of his book that attacked the church and Christians, "If all the Christians I know had been like Aunt Hattie, this book would never have been written." A compliment to a great Christian lady. A condemnation to an uncaring church.

CONCLUSION

I am going to ask you to do something positive in helping you to get ready for your own spiritual renewal. I am going to ask the church leaders to come and touch this altar as a commitment that you are willing to put yourself on the altar for God's use, every day in some way to share Him with any lost person He allows you to meet. I ask the musicians to play quietly with every head bowed, all eyes closed, and every heart yielded unto the Lord. This is praying time.
This is dedicating time.
This is confession time.

This is a time between you and your God. Are you ready to follow Him?

"Spiritual sclerosis is a deadly build-up of sin that resists the flow of God's power and purpose in your life."

THE HARDENING OF THE HEART

Hebrews 3:7-19

1. Dr. Herbert Beeler wrote a book titled <u>Food Is Your Medicine.</u> He states the # 1 killer in America is heart failure. Every time you breathe, someone, somewhere, suffers a heart attack that often results in death. Many of these attacks are caused by cholesterol, a disease called "arterial sclerosis," a build-up of a fatty substance that slowly closes the blood-carrying arteries, interfering with the flow of blood to vital organs. When these bits of fat flake off in the arteries, they can cause either a coronary or a cerebral heart attack: Coronary affects the heart. Cerebral affects the brain.

2. Now I tell you that, not to give a lecture on medicine, but to point you to an interesting parallel found in the Word of God. <u>Read Hebrews 3:7-19.</u> The Greek word for "hardening" is the medical word "sclerosis." And spiritual sclerosis is a deadly build-up of sin that resists the flow of God's power and purpose through your life.

3. Note verse 13, it tells us to "exhort one another daily." Pray for one another, encourage one another and help one another. WHY? "Lest any of you" allow yourself to become hardened against compassion; or, failure in caring and sharing God's love with one another. To fail here is to cut yourself off from God's flowing supply of help and healing. Since this is not only possible, but probable, I want us to consider the "Hardening of the Heart."

Three observations: 1. The CURSE of the hardened Heart.
       2. The CAUSE of the hardened heart.
       3. The CURE for the hardened heart.
(I think this outline came from one of our pastors)

I. THE CURSE OF THE HEARDENED HEART

1. The Bible always equates human nature, apart from God, as being corruptive.

**David: "In sin did my mother conceive me." Psalm 51:5. Meaning, sin was already abiding in her nature, and it was passed along to him.

**The Apostle Paul wrote, "In my flesh dwelleth no good thing." Rom. 7:18.

**I read an article written by Dr. Stanley Sakabu, Director of Trauma at St. John's Medical Center in St. Louis, Mo. "America has a heart problem today...the abandonment as a culture of the idea that human life is sacred. That human beings are created (by) God, whose right alone it is to determine the number of their days." He refers to the former days when school children settled their differences by fussing; and the extreme then was to have fistfights. Now they resolve differences with knives and guns. The slow hardening, desensitizing of human values, is reaching into our younger generations."

2. And if human nature is to be to any advantage, it must be overmastered by the Divine nature. And this happens only when the once born become the twice born by Divine regeneration. "Ye must be born again." John 3:7

3. Spiritual sclerosis, hardening of the heart, begins when we allow the old nature to slowly move back into our thinking, into our doing, and becoming habitual blockages to a growing spiritual life.

Note the conflict of the natural and the supernatural in Rom. 7:23-24. Some of us will have to admit there were former days when our hearts were more tender than they are right now.
> We were more open to God's bidding.
> We were aware of needs in people around us.
> We enjoyed sweet fellowship with God's children.

We found it easy to weep over spiritual problems.

But today, things that used to bother us, don't trouble us anymore.

**One psychologist says, "The greatest need is this, they don't know how to cry anymore." The curse of the hardened heart. And if that is true of people outside the church, what about those inside the church? This is the warning that is echoed in Heb. 3:8, 13.

**G. Campbell Morgan, "You once cried over the death of a pet canary. But now you don't even cry over the deaths of lost souls." You can put a new label on it and call it "sophistication," "maturity," or "adjustment." But I don't buy that, and I doubt if God buys that. "A rose by any other name would smell just as sweet." And, "A skunk by any other name would cause just as much stink."

Why do we no longer weep over our sins and the lostness of others? Why do we no longer read the Bible with enthusiasm and expectancy?
Why do you no longer pray as you once prayed? A hardened heart might be responsible.

Look with me at:

Number 1. The rebellion in this curse.

(a) <u>Stubbornness:</u>   Heb.3:10 "They do always err in their heart." They are determined to do their own thing.

   — In Egypt the children of Israel had witnessed God's interven-
     tion with plagues to help set them free from enslavement.
   —They saw God divide the sea for Israel and close it on Pharaoh
     and His army.
   —They were fed daily with manna from Heaven.

In spite of all that, God said of them: "They knew not my ways, they would not discern my ways." verse 10. How about you? You've known God's power and presence in the past. Remember your conversion? The overwhelming peace you felt in your heart. Remember your concern for the lost. Your heart was stirred by messages from God. You weren't critical of the preacher's grammar as long as he preached to the needs of your heart from the Bible. You weren't afraid of the devil nor death. But somewhere along the line you cooled off. You slowly lost enthusiasm. Your actions, or non-actions, shut down God's power in and through your life? You no longer tuned into what God was doing and what He was saying. You began to doubt if God really is working in your life and the lives of other people. Stubbornness leads to (b) Rebellion. "As in the days of provocation." v 8. In those days they rebelled against Aaron. Israel rebelled against Moses. They rebelled against God over big things and little things. And it can happen to you. When you get too busy to read and study God's Word. When you allow "ME" and "MINE" to become greater in your agenda.

- When your conversation becomes worldly and does not honor God.

- When you offend someone who is precious to the Lord.

Do you condone, and conduct, certain indulgences you wouldn't do if Jesus were standing by your side? Are you too critical of people, and becoming more critical? Do you grumble and complain more than you try to encourage? Is your worship still worshipful, and meaningful? Any of the above is a tell-tale sign of spiritual sclerosis, and a warning to make it right; otherwise, it tends to worsen.

God has said, "Forsake not the assembly." Don't miss church without a valid reason. God has said, "Pray without ceasing." Supplication, Intervention, Praise! And if these things are not in your life consistently, this is your "day of provocation."

Number 2: Another cause resulting from the hardened heart is: Impatience: One day Israel put up her tents. The next day she took down her tents. Num. 14:29, God told them, "Your carcasses will fall in this wilderness." They would not be allowed to reach the Promised Land, God's goal for them. How many started the journey from Egypt? No one knows for sure. It is estimated anywhere from 600 thousand up to 3 million. How many of them entered Canaan Land? There were only two adults who began the trip, Joshua and Caleb, along with the younger ones born during the 40 years in the wilderness. The older ones died because they doubted God. They suffered the curse of the hardened heart.

II. BUT WHAT CAUSED THE HARDENED HEART?

See Heb. 3: 13 b, "The deceitfulness of sin."

1. It always begins with <u>doubting God's Word.</u> Gen.3:3, "Yea, hath God said?" Satan: "God might have said it, but you don't have to believe it."

(Burton version)

This is really the greatest issue among some theologians today. "Did God really say that?" "Does God really mean that?" "Why there's no fish ever been seen that could swallow and take care of a fleeing prophet for three days." So says some not-so-smart people who believe God has to work within their own limited framework of knowledge and understanding. I ask, Who created the greatest whale in the ocean? I answer, "God did." And I add, He could have made a fish to swallow that fish."

But this kind of questioning creates questions and doubt about God's creation and God's Word. A problem when some genius rises up and says, "There are some spots that are spurious in the Bible." And that sentence implies God has appointed them to spot those spots. DUH?

How many people are present who really believe a soul is lost without Jesus Christ? I'll tell you how many. They are the ones who are attempting to help reach the lost who are doomed if somebody doesn't reach them. "Be ye doers of the Word, and not hearers only." James 1:22

2. The "deceitfulness of sin" continues when you listen and believe the devil's lies. (See Genesis 3:5) Some years ago Dr. Joseph Fletcher introduced "situational ethics" and the "God is dead" theory. And people, not well founded in the Bible, thought it might be so. If you haven't seen it lately, this concept has grown and is being thrust upon gullible people in the social religion sector now called, "Secular Humanism. Their philosophy: Man's thoughts are greater than God's Word. Man, with proper training and discipline, can become gods.

People in Eden's garden can defy God's command, but they shall surely die. This is validated every day in hundreds of funerals and cremations. People in today's society can doubt God's truth, but they shall surely suffer for it. People in the pews can attempt to create their own brand of salvation, but they shall die in their sins if Jesus Christ is not their personal Saviour

When anyone doubts God's Word and denies God's truth, and defy God's will, that person will pay the price for his doubt, denial and defiance. Hebrews 10:31, "It is a fearful thing to fall into the hands of the living God." It is for the unbeliever and the unbelieving.

"God is not mocked, for whatsoever a man soweth, that shall he also reap." Sin, doubt and disobedience are registered in Heaven. It shows up on earth in your countenance, in your eyes, in speech, and in your body language.

    -It affects your blood pressure.
    -It limits your days on the earth.
    -It extends suffering beyond this life.

But I will not leave you in this hopeless, helpless, hellish situation. God has a hope and He has a help. Let's look at it in

III. THE CURE FOR THE HARDENED HEART

(See Heb. 3:7, 8, 12)
1. The cure comes by hearing and heeding the "His voice." v7

**Little Susie was riding cross-country on a pullman train with her parents. At bedtime, young Susie was in a berth across the aisle from her mother. After tucking her in, Mom kissed Susie goodnight and closed the curtain. About five minutes later Susie became afraid, and called to her mother. "Mother, are you there?" "Yes, Susie, I am here." A few minutes later she called to her daddy in the upper berth, "Daddy, are you there?" "Yes, Susie, I am here." Ten minutes later, "Mother are you still there?" "Yes, Susie." A while later, "Daddy, are you still there?" A tired businessman responded, "Yes, Susie, your mom is here, your Dad is here. I am here. Everybody is here. Now go to sleep." A few minutes later, a tiny voice, whispered, "Mother, was that God?"

God speaks in many ways to us:
He speaks to us through a sermon, through a trusted friend, through prayer, through happenings around us, through nature, through good books. And especially through the Holy Spirit speaking to our conscience. But He primarily speaks to all of us through His Word. Often the barometer of your faith is your quiet time with the Lord. If you do not now have a time to be alone with God, begin one immediately. If you do this regularly, it won't be long until your heart will be tender, If you do this regularly, it won't be long until your spirit will take wings. And until you do, I ask this question, which is more harmful, professing atheism? or, practicing atheism? Either leads to a hardening of the heart.

2. Not only hear God's Word, but heed God's Word. Stress verse 12: "Take heed brethren, lest there be in any of you an evil heart of unbelief." You might be getting a warning from the Lord today. No doubt about it, if you have let your personal relationship with the Lord and His people cool, you are in need of immediate radical repair. The call is to you! The warning is to you. If you don't heed

the warning, then you will get to a point where you simply don't care. A symptom of a hardened heart.

CONCLUSION

But you can be cured! Do you want a cure? Listen for God's voice. Obey His leading. The cure will come! Ask God to let it happen for you right now. Amen

"God has a plan for the family, and when that plan is implemented, the family works."

THE HEAD OF THE HOME

Ephesians 5:15-27

Dr. Joyce Brothers made a startling statement that rattled my cage, and it should make every thinking person question whether she might be correct. She said "Marriage is a 'quiet hell' for one half of the families in America."

I wondered if she was responding to valid scientific information she had gathered; or, was this her personal assumption after counseling so many dysfunctional families.

Current statistics bear out the fact that divorce mills are operating at one-half times the marriage mills. One of two marriages are on the rocks and end in divorce.

W must be quick to sound the alarm found in Psalm 11:3, "If the (basic) foundations be destroyed, what can the righteous do?" My answer to that is Vince Lombardi's challenge to a failing team, "Get back to the basics that work." God has given us formulas that are structured to maintain a stable society. In His planning we are to have a home for every phase of our being:

— He has provided a home for our birth.
— He has made provision for the home of our marriage.
— He has provided the church, the home of our faith,
— And to complete this home emphasis, He has provided Heaven, the home of our future.

Also He has given us a formula and outline for successful homes.
1. The Christian father is to be the head of the home.
2. The Christian mother is to be the heart of the home.
3. And children are to be helpers in the home.

Number 1 above is today's subject for our Message with a Mission. Read Ephesians 5:15-29

**Years ago I heard a brother preacher, Dr. Samson from Detroit, say, "In the beginning God made Adam. And when God took a good look at Adam, He said to Himself, 'Surely I can do better than that' - then He made Eve." He went on to say that Eve was completed to complement Adam. And Adam was to complement and complete Eve.

The problem in the home begins to increase when members start to quarrel over their "rights" and stop yielding to their God-given roles. When this happens, everybody in the home begins to lose foundational stability. This I know for sure, any time the head on the body, or the heart in the body gets confused about their proper roles, that person is headed for serious consequences. It is equally true when the head of the home and the heart of the home are uncertain about their God-given roles, they are headed for trouble within the family structure. Thus, society, and especially Christians, must get back to our standard. God has a plan for the family, and when that implemented, the family works!

Remember! Man is three dimensional in his God-given role:
  1. He is a biological creation.
  2. He is a sociological creation.
  3. He is a theological creation.

All of these parts of man's being must enter and become involved in the marriage scene. Any one of these, without considering the other is incomplete.

1. **Biologically**, husbands are to be partners with the wife and God in the creation of new human life. Marriage must be based upon more than fulfilling sexual satisfaction. If sex is primary in a union, it is little more than animal attraction for the opposite sex. And this kind of marriage is already headed for the rocks and ruin.

2. As a **sociological** creature, man is under pressure from society to conform to its standards. Thus, a man can be trapped because he entered into marriage for the wrong reason. He might marry because it is expected that a normal man will want to wed and begin his own family. Some men marry for business reasons. Some marry for economic gain:

> SHE: "You married me because Daddy left me a lot of money."
> HE: "I would have married you no matter who left you the money."

Basically, a man will marry because he needs a woman to complete him, just as most women need a man to complete her.

**This is not to discredit the unmarrieds. There are thousands who fit into God's Kingdom who choose never to marry.

> HE: "Will you marry me?"
> SHE: "No," — And they both lived happily ever after.

Recall the situation in Eden: "God saw that it was not good for the man to be alone, so He created a help-mate for Adam." Gen.2:18, "And for this cause," says Jesus, "shall a man leave his father and mother and cleave unto his wife." Matt.19:5. I believe the best glue to hold the marriage together through any difficulty is Commitment. Commitment will see a couple through after romantic loves begins to wane.

3. Then there is the **theological** reason for marriage. This is God's design. A spiritual triangle relationship includes God, husband and wife. "Except the Lord build the house, they labor in vain that build it." Ps. 27:1. A marriage can be expected to endure highs and lows when these three truths are factored into the marriage equation, the biological, the sociological and the theological.

Marriages that are not made in Heaven have to be made somewhere else. And I cringe to think where some are made. (That is why I refuse to marry a Christian to a non-Christian) "Be not unequally yoked together with unbelievers." 2 Cor. 6:14. If I perform a wedding ceremony, the couple must promise to begin their marriage with a Christian home, "With God as their Father, Christ as their Saviour, and the Holy Spirit as their daily Helper." And the marriage that comes closest to the ideal is a marriage that is Bible-centered and God-controlled. Men! If your marriage is not Bible-centered and God controlled, then you disqualify yourself from being head of the home as God wants and wills for you to be.

Allow me to show you three simple elements that the head of the home must be, must do, and must give.

I. THE HEAD OF THE HOME MUST BE A CHRISTIAN

And this is far more than simply belonging to a church. I have a sermon on What is a real Christian?"

1. A real Christian is <u>BORN RIGHT</u>. Jesus told a very religious man, "Ye must be born again." There is no way you can be a member of God's family without undergoing the new birth!

2. A real Christian is <u>FED RIGHT</u>. The Bible says to all Christians, "Feed on the Word." What food is to the nurture of the body, the Word is to the nurture of the soul.

3. A real Christian is <u>LED RIGHT</u>. He is led by the Holy Spirit in all his decisions and his directions.

4. A real Christian also <u>LIVES RIGHT</u>. It is impossible to be a holy Christian at the Lord's Table on Sunday and then be a holy terror at the breakfast table with burned toast on Monday. God knows the difference. People know the difference and you know the difference.

5. A real Christian <u>DIES RIGHT</u>. He dies knowing that he is going to be with Christ and God's family forevermore. This is his trust. This is his destiny.

II. THE HEAD OF THE HOUSE MUST HAVE A HEALTHY PASSION AND COMPASSION FOR HIS MATE.

Hear again the directive in Eph.5:25, "Husbands, love your wives." When your wife submits to you as head of the home, then you must respond to this submission with Godly love.

The Bible does not say,   "Husband, berate your wife."
                          Nor " Husband, browbeat your wife,"
                          Nor, "Husband, intimidate your wife."

As head in the home, you must love her. And how? 25b "As Christ loved the church." This includes sanctity, and sacrifice. Now that is a spiritual demand with a special dimension. Don't you dare to throw verses 5:22-24 at her without including verse 25.

Men, when you dare to put some real love and compassion into your marriage, you'll be delighted at the returns you get. Proverbs 15:17, "Better is a dinner of herbs where love is, than a stalled ox and hatred therewith." Meaning: It's better to have turnip greens with love than to have T-bone steak where there is turmoil. That was spoken by a man who had 300 wives and 700 concubines. But before you get excited by that fact, remember this, he also had 300 mothers-in-law. Men, no matter which direction the psychologists and sociologists try to reconstruct the foundation of the family, make sure your family is founded upon God's teachings. This will guarantee you a good and durable home.

**Dr. Paul Popenoe, of the American Institute of Family Relations, says there are seven barriers that a husband might stumble over all the way from the altar to the grave.

LACK OF TENDERNESS headed the list. I saw an outstanding love sign one day: The message read, "Lee Loves Dee." It was spray-painted on a dumpster at a roadside. "Why preacher, that's foolish, I'd never do a thing like that." Of course you wouldn't, because you would be more afraid of what people may say than what you want your mate to think. But guess what, this was a wonderful statement to Dee about Lee's love for her.

Another thing in a husband's relationship with his wife, both have warts. And if you major in fault-finding, counting warts, you will minor in the major things of importance in the marriage. I use a portion of I Cor. 13 in my marriage vows. And I use the New English Version that states, "Love keeps no score of wrongs." Beautiful! You don't keep any negative scores when the Head of the Home is the Christian model in the home.

The final thing:
1. Be a Christian husband and Dad.
2. Have a healthy passion and compassion for your mate.

III. AND THREE: GIVE PROPER CORRECTION AND DIRECTION TO YOUR CHILDREN

We are living in a day when everything is controlled by switches, except the children. In my own lifetime I have lived to see psychology swing back and forth in regards to child rearing. It is apparent to me that some of these professionals have never raised, nor reared children.

To spank or not to spank, that might be the question. Prov. 13:24, "He that spareth his rod hateth his son." Living Bible translation: "If you refuse to discipline your son, it proves you don't love him (in the right way.) For, if you love him, you will be prompt to punish him." That opens up a can of worms. It means this: If your child is doing something that will be hurtful to himself, or hurtful to someone else. Stop him from doing it right now. If you don't, the act will become a habit. And a habit is much more difficult to correct than a single act. Some parents have had to learn "tough love" for tough children.

You either teach a child what he must do, or the child will teach you he is going to do what he chooses to do when he wants to do it. The case rests in your court. Years ago Dr. John Holland gave this challenge to fathers:

"Fathers: Play with your children
     Stay with your children
     Pray with your children." CASE CLOSED!!!

CONCLUSION

**Dr. George Truett was pastor of First Baptist in Dallas, Texas, for many years. He preached on the family one night and challenged each father to have a time of prayer and devotion together. A business man came to the altar and confessed: "Pastor, I've lived miserably far from what is right and consistent. Family prayer will be at my house tonight and every night from this day on. "Next morning Dr. Truett was on his way to his study at the church. He saw the businessman's sixteen-year old son awaiting him. He told Dr. Truett, "You should have been at our house last night. Daddy called us into the den and apologized to us that he had not been the Christian father that he needed to be. He cried and we cried with him. Then he knelt down and prayed. I went to my room, but couldn't sleep. I realized I was not a genuine Christian. I ask you now to help me to find Jesus Christ as my Saviour." Glory!!! Next Sunday morning the boy responded to the altar call. Dr. Truett: "Tell us, my boy, what started you on the upward way towards Christ?" The boy looked across the pews at his dad and said, "It was Dad's prayer last Sunday night." Dads! Did you get what that son said about his Dad?

Isaiah 38:19, "The father of the children shall make known the truth." In our day, when one-half of the burglaries are committed by young people, dad, MAKE GOD'S TRUTH KNOWN TO YOUR CHILDREN! "Thou shalt not steal." In our day when Americans spend twice as much for alcohol than on all religion, charities and schools combined, Dad, MAKE GOD'S TRUTH KNOWN TO YOUR CHILDREN. "Abstain from every appearance of evil." I Thess. 5:22. In our country where children are no better because their parents are no better, <u>MAKE GOD'S TRUTH KNOWN TO YOUR CHILDREN</u>. Instruct them to follow people only who follow God!

I know some of the pressures you face in family life. How can I make God's truth known to my children when we sit down at the table, and somebody never fails to say in some way, "Let's rush through the meal so we can rush somewhere else." <u>Head of the Home</u>, remember that your child is growing into a rose, or he is growing into something else. And it is mainly up to you which direction he grows!

THREE THINGS FOR CHRISTIAN FATHERS:

    I. Be a Christian.
    2. Have passion and compassion for your mate.
    3. Give proper correction and Direction to your children.

Each one of these is a special relationship (1) With God.
                                          (2) With your mate.
                                          (3) With your child.

DO IT!

"There's life in a look."

BEHOLD, THE LAMB

John 1:29

**Josephus was a Jewish historian who lived between 37 AD and 97AD. He was born in the same decade that Jesus Christ died. He wrote in his journals, "There was about this time, Jesus, a wise man,if it be lawful to call him a man. For he was a doer of wonderful works, a teacher. He drew over to him many of the Jews and many of the Gentiles. He was Christ, and when Pilate had condemned him to a cross, those that loved him at the first did not forsake him. For he appeared to them alive again the third day, as the divine prophets had foretold these, and ten thousand other wonderful things concerning him, and the tribe of Christians so named for him, are not extinct to this day."

Hear this letter by Publius Lintulus to the Roman senate describing Jesus: "Man of stature somewhat tall, his hair the color of a chestnut, fully ripe...curling and waving about his shoulders; his forehead plain and very delicate, his beard thick in color like his hair. His eyes gray, quick and clear."

Now listen to one other testimony by a living witness - Read John 1:29-34

1. John, the Baptist was a N.T. prophet and preacher. He refused to go into Jerusalem among the priests and pharisees; rather, he preached in the wilderness so mightily that the townspeople came out to hear him. His diet and dress were somewhat peculiar - clothed in camel's hair, he ate locusts (grasshoppers) and wild honey. He was an unusual man, using the banks of the Jordan River for a pulpit, he thundered his sermon with two primary points:

    (a) "Repent of the sins that condemn you."

    (b) "Receive Jesus Christ as Redeemer to save you from
        condemnation."

His message echoed through mountains and valleys. They continue down through the valleys of time to this very day: "Behold the Lamb of God Who takes away the sin of the world." His audience understood that language. They had taken thousands of innocent sheep to the temple to be sacrificed for their own guilt and sin. The Jews knew their theology well, that sin and disobedience to God caused moral compromise, judgment and death. They also knew God's only way of atonement, cleansing from sin, was the vicarious death of the innocent for the guilty. In Exodus 12, they had instructions concerning the Passover lamb. Verse 3, "They shall take to them every man a lamb." Verse 5. "The "lamb shall be without blemish." Verse 6, "Keep it (penned) until the 14th day of the month; and before the whole assembly of Israel shall ye kill it in the evening." They were instructed to place some of the sheep's blood over the lentil of the door. And this promise in verse 13, "When I see the blood, I will pass over you." "I WILL SPARE YOU OF MY WRATH!"

Oh dear believer, did you hear that? Listen again. On that great getting up morning, God, the Judge, when He sees you, He will know that you have been covered by the blood of Lamb, and He will declare that you are righteous, that you are redeemed! And you will know it too, the angels will know it, and all other saints will know it because you will be wearing the regal garment like unto God's only begotten Son!

PRAISES BE UNTO JESUS CHRIST WHO PAID FOR ALL YOUR SIN, HE PAID THE DEBT FOR ALL YOUR SHAME, JESUS PAID IT ALL, ALL, ALL! Amen and Amen.

Behold, the Lamb!

2. Qualifications for the Paschal lamb were three:
    (a) It had to be young (innocent).
    (b) It had to be male.

(c) It had to be free from any marks or defects.

(d) Jesus was 33 years young.

(e) Jesus was a male.

(f) Jesus was perfect and stainless. God's selected Lamb!

John the Baptist saw this fulfillment in Jesus Christ. And it was to his delight to point to Jesus, and tell the crowd, "Behold, the Lamb." God's Paschal Lamb. God's special Lamb. Jesus met all of the required specifications. This is why the Apostle Paul could tell people through the ages that, "God hath made Christ, Who knew no sin, to be sin for us, that we may be made the righteousness of God in Him." Do you have any doubts about that? Are you struggling with your faith? Do you let satan whisper to your soul that you are unworthy? Are you a crippled spirit trying to find enough strength within yourself to make it all the way to glory?

Let me tell you something loud and clear. You cannot ever do anything, <u>absolutely nothing</u>, to earn your way into Heaven. You must trust the Lamb to cover your past, to control your present and to confirm your future. You must stop trying to justify your salvation by any good works you have done; and, You must start trusting completely what Jesus Christ, the Lamb, has done to make it possible for you to have an abundant life, and to enjoy eternal life.

That is the pure Gospel! That is why we pray, and preach, and proclaim it to others. Jesus died once for your sins. He won't die anymore! And once you have trusted Jesus to save you, it is done! It is complete! It is forever!

**Bishop Gerald Kennedy defines his preaching mission this way, "I do not know what concious aim other preachers have in preaching. For me, it is to proclaim a conviction about God's nature, God's will, God's promises, God's resources and God's power. It is to bear testimony to the truth of Christ, and to help people see themselves as the objects of God's love revealed in Christ." WELL SAID!

My Soul! If we see that, and understand that, and accept that truth, how can believers come into this sanctuary with stooped shoulders, shuffling feet and defeated spirits? "Lift up your heads, o ye gates, and be ye lifted up, ye everlasting doors, and the King of Glory shall come in."

He is here! And when you receive Him,
He will lift your spirits,
He will forgive your failures.
He will defeat your enemies.
He will solve your problems.
He will ease your pain.
He will overcome your weakness.

He will secure your future.

Praise unto the Lamb of God, and Jesus Christ is His name.

I guess I have already preached. But the above is a prelude to three truths rising out of our text:

I. BEHOLD THE LAMB: SEE HIS MAJESTY.

1. Listen to Phil. 2:9-11 (read) In this day when nothing seems holy to unholy men, we who know the Lord of lords and King of all kings, we must lift Him up for all to see:

> Lift Him up in our daily speech,
> Lift Him up in our daily walk,
> Lift Him up in our daily work,
> Lift Him up in our daily witness.

And we will do that when we learn to lift Him up in daily worship! As Moses lifted up the serpent in the wilderness, even so must the Son of man be lifted up, that whosoever believeth in Him shall not perish, but have eternal life."

Let your desk, or your toolbox, or wherever you work, let this be your pulpit to proclaim to dying people around you that there is an alternative, an escape from plunging into darkness and eternal defeat and death. There is hope for them. There is a Redeemer, a Saviour. Share with them what the Lord has done for you.

**Norman Gulley, in the Washington Review and Herald, wrote: "Surely America stumbles headlong toward the final prespice, tripped on the downward road of immorality. It plunges with ever increasing momentum toward the point of no return."

Pulpiteering with a pen!

2. Beloved brothers and sisters - It could be that yours is the only candle burning for the Lord that your co-workers will see. You may not be allowed to let your light shine in Washington, or Russia, or China; but you can, and you must let it shine wherever you work, wherever you live, wherever you play.

That people in spiritual darkness will see in you, and through you, the One Who is the Light of the world! People without redemption desperately need to see Jesus Christ, and for so many people who will never see Him through the preached Word from a pulpit, they need to see Him walking in your shoes, speaking through your lips, loving through your heart.

We have enough believers in this church, in this town, to woo and to witness, to witness and to win, all the unsaved within our communities. When we allow Jesus Christ to rule and reign, to reach and redeem people through our committed witnessing.

Why don't we do it?
Why has Christ been thrown out of schools?
Why are born-again Christians fast becoming a minority?
Why are so many churches being abandoned by its members?

There is a simple answer: Too many church members have taken their eyes off the Lamb of God and are focusing them on something else. And that produces failure!

**The apostle Peter did that, and he sank instead of walking tall on the water at Christ's command. And it can happen to you when you takle your eyes off the Person of miraculous supply to the problems of a merciless sea.

3. Please listen to me. You are only as strong as your power source.

    —When you keep plugged in to your problems.
    —When you focus on your weaknesses,
    —When you excuse service to God because of your limitations,

You will never walk in peace and freedom on the waters of faith.
You will never be positive in your testimony to Christ's majesty
You will never communicate to others,   "Behold the Lamb.
                                  Receive the Lamb.
                                  Follow the Lamb."

UNTIL you validate that witness when you daily behold the Lamb.
    When you, by concious effort, hold on to the Lamb daily.
        When daily you follow the Lamb.

4. Dear saint of God, when you magnify Christ with your life and your lips, you will have resources to turn your tragedies into triumph.
        Your scars into stars.
        Your defeat into success.
        Your worries into wonders,

And He will enable you to help turn sinners into saints. Focus your eyes on Christ. Forget those pressing circumstances. Christ is Master of winds without, and wars within the soul.

Turn your eyes upon Jesus, and keep your eyes upon Jesus when you do this, you will become a Victor instead of a victim. "Behold the Lamb!"

II. SEE HIS MAJESTY AND APPROPRIATE HIS MERCY

"Behold the Lamb." Hold fast to His proffered mercy.

1. Satan has a lot of Christians crippled and defeated by getting them to think, "Yes, there was a time when Jesus forgave me - but since then I have been tempted, I yielded, and have stumbled over and over again." Thus nullifying, for them, a positive witness of Christ's permanent keeping power.

It is a fact that we stumble from time to time. We will when the flesh is allowed to dominate our spirit. But hear this promise in Ps. 37:23-24, and hear it well: "The steps of a good man (believer) are ordered by the Lord, and God delighteth in his way. Though he fall, he SHALL NOT BE UTTERLY CAST DOWN, for the Lord upholdeth him." Do you not agree that it is OK for the Lord to pick you up when you fall, to hold you and keep you from falling into eternal perdition? That is what He will do. His mercy is a lasting, unchanging mercy. He can't change it because of Who He is. You can't change it by what you do. Lam. 3:22, "It is of the Lord's mercies that we are not consumed, because His compassions fail not." We fail. He never fails!

> The soul that on Jesus hath leaned for repose,
> I will not, I will not desert to his foes.
> That soul, though all hell should endeavor to shake,
> I'll never, no never, no never forsake!
> —John Rippon

2. Let me help you if you are one of those members who is always stumbling. What if every morning when you leave your house, you stumbled over a big rock that was directly in your pathway. You did this daily until your toes screamed out in pain. What should you do? Need I tell you? For sanity's sake,

> For peace of mind,
> For escaping further injury? Get it resolved!

You must do one of two things: Either move that rock out of your pathway, or find another way to get to where you are going.

If some sin, some problem is causing you, or someone else to be hurt, if you feel wounded and overcome, if you have come to the place where you cannot handle it, You do have another recourse. You do have an avenue of victory. You must turn it over to Him Who says, "My grace is sufficient for you. My strength is made perfect in your weakness." Hell has never forged a chain that Jesus Christ cannot break!

It is time to turn your weakness over to His mercy. About 5 years ago, my son-in-law had a stroke. It left him unable to read anything with understanding. The words would reverse themselves. He would avoid reading anything. This past Christmas, my daughter bought him a Bible. Once again, he tried to read it, and he became frustrated. Sharon told him, "Sal, why don't you ask Jesus to help you to read it with understanding." "OK, I guess I will." She told him, "Ask Jesus to do it right now." Sal prayed. Sal is now in Bible study and reading his Bible every day.

3. O Listen, "The Lord is good, His mercy is everlasting." It goes on and on. It goes i1nto the hearts of ancient Israel, into the spirits of N.T. saints, into Martin Luther, into Billy Graham. And God is waiting just to give it to you, again and again.

    a. Before you prayed your first prayer, His mercy was everlasting. After you have prayed your last prayer, His mercy is everlasting.

    b. Before you shedded your first tear, His mercy was everlasting. After you have shedded your last tear, His mercy is everlasting

c. Before you committed your first sin, His mercy was everlasting. After you have committed your last sin, His mercy is everlasting.

d. Before you were born, His mercy was everlasting. After you are dead and gone from this world, His mercy is still everlasting.

"Everything then depends on God's mercy, and not what people want to do." Rom.9:16. Romans 9:15, "I will have mercy on whom I will have mercy."

It is God's option to give you His mercy.

It is man's opportunity to reach out in faith and receive it.

"Behold the Lamb."

III. SEE HIS MAJESTY APPROPRIATE HIS MERCY. THIS WILL EFFECT YOUR MINISTRY FOR HIM.

**Let me illustrate this with a true story.

1. There is a young lady who works in the sheriff's office in another county in South Carolina. This young, single woman lived mainly for herself. She spent her money on things for herself. She is the daughter of my daughter's friend.

One December the Sheriff's Department found a poor woman living with her two small children. The mother was wasting away with cancer. There was very little food found in the home. The children wore dirty, ragged clothing. This young woman heard about this mother and her two kids. She decided to visit in that home. And when she saw all the deprivation, she went to the market and bought a load of groceries for that family. She became an advocate and raised money for them to have gifts at Christmas. When she took the gifts and saw the unbelievable appreciation, she later said, "This the best Christmas I have ever had."

2. This is the effect of God's love working through people to touch needy people.

> This girl went to the place of need.
> She then gave to relieve the need.
> This is ministry.

And this is what every church member ought to be doing. Find someone in need and respond to that need with God's love.

3. When believers learn to reach up to God with one hand, and then reach out to needy people with the other hand; then, and only then do they fall in love with ministering for Jesus. "Inasmuch as ye have done it unto one of the least of these, my brethren, ye have done it unto me." says Jesus.

CONCLUSION

Today, be sure that you take a good look to see the majestic Christ. And do not fail to ask for, and receive His mercy. This will lead you to get involved in His ministry. And ministry for Christ can happen any time, any place.

**A Hospice Physician in Denver, Colo., tells this story. He was on a busy thoroughfare headed home. His vehicle sputtered. He drove ino a near-by Quick Mart. He started to call a tow truck. A woman stumbled out of the store. He got out of his car to help her. She was sobbing. She dropped a nickel. He picked it up. He saw her car was piled with children and stuff. He asked, "May I help you?" She told him she had to give up her apartment, and she was now on her way to California to live with her parents. "Were you just now praying?" asked the doctor. She backed away from this strange man. He told her, "He heard you, and He sent me."

He took out a card and swiped it through the gas payment machine. While he was gassing up her car, he walked over to a near-by McDonald's and bought a sack full of burgers and fries, and also some additional gift certificates. The children grabbed the bag and began to eat. He said, "I gave her my gloves, a quick hug, and prayed for her safety while she traveled on the road." As she began pulling away, she asked him, "Are you an angel, or something?" "I shed some tears, and told her. No, angels are busy during these days before Christmas, so sometimes God uses regular people." When he got into his car, it cranked without a sputter. He said, "I'll put it in the shop tomorrow, but I bet the mechanic won't find anything wrong with it."

God uses regular people - that is, when regular people are willing to do something special for the Lord." Amen

"Something always comes up to betray the man who professes to be what he is not.""

KILL THOSE CAPTURED SHEEP

1 Samuel 15:1-9

Out in the mid-west a woman boarded a plane to go visit her parents. Unknown to her, her husband had taken out a large insurance policy on her. And that fatal day she carried a time bomb on board with her luggage. After the plane was air-borne, the bomb exploded and many lives were lost. Later the husband admitted his crime.

Many Christians are traveling from here to eternity with excess luggage that threatens their journey. The sermon today will explain what I mean.

1. Saul, the first king of Israel was a tragic figure. (No man ever got off to a better beginning, and few men have had such an inglorious ending.) The Living Bible says "Saul was the most handsome man in Israel." 1 Sam. 9:2. Girls, did you know that Saul was tall, dark and handsome? The Lord makes a good-looking guy once in a while to break the monotony

Saul was a strong man in many ways, yet he was weak in one important virtue where he needed to be strong, and that was in obedience to the Lord.

2. God had used Saul and his army to punish the Amalakites, the ancient enemy who often made unprovoked attacks upon Israel. Before the battle had begun, the Lord had ordered the total extermination of the Amalek people, their possessions, and their king. When Saul and his army conquered the Amalakites, he disobeyed the Lord by sparing King Agag, and he also spared some choice sheep and cattle from Ai, the capital city of Amalek.

3. But Samuel, God's prophet, turned up at the right moment, and Saul had to think quickly of something religious to say. "Samuel came to Saul, and Saul said unto him, 'Blessed be thou of the Lord: I have performed the commandment of the Lord.'"

Those lying words had hardly been spoken when those captured sheep started bleating, and the oxen bellowed. Samuel demanded, "What meaneth then this bleating of the sheep in mine ears? And the lowing of oxen which I hear?" Listen, something always comes up to betray the man who professes to be what he is not. Whether he be king of commoner, President or peasant. The sheep we should have slaughtered will bleat at the most inopportune time, and show up the farce that chatter cannot conceal.

4. Saul kept that which God told him to destroy. Excess baggage. And the person who insists on holding on to idols, temptations, bad habits and affections that God has commanded to exterminate, will stand condemned by those very things on some day of judgment. And the worst things about our sins, is that they find us out, and show us up! Sin is a dangerous game that nobody wins. Nobody! Numbers 32:23, "Be sure your sin will find you out." That does not necessarily mean that others will discover your private sin, but it does means the sin itself will make its mark upon your life and attitudes. The LB says, "Your sin will catch up with you." It's been said by many preachers, "You can't sin and win."

**I was preaching along these lines in a revival in Alabama. I stated that sin will create physical problems. It can cause illness. Headaches. It can cause your blood pressure to rise. When I said that, there was some laughing in the congregation. Later I was told the pastor was having problems with high blood pressure. Well!

Sin is never in a hurry. But sooner or later it will serve you with a summons to appear before the bar of conscience - and it becomes a star witness against you.

5. The same God Who used a donkey to bring Baalim to his senses. The same God Who used a rooster to bring Peter to repentant tears, Is the same God Who used bleating sheep to expose the wrong-doing of a disobedient king. And this same God will use any means to expose our hidden sins, in order for us to deal with them, admit their wrongness, that we might repent and be restored to fellowship with Him.

6. It is possible somebody here is burdened because you are weighted down under some excess baggage. And you know God has told you to get rid of it. And because you have been unwilling to deal with it, your spiritual life is in turmoil. You no longer enjoy true worship. Fellowship with other Christians causes conviction in your spirit.

> Thus prayers are unprayed,
> The Bible remains unread.
> Tithes remain ungiven.

Somewhere in a yesterday, you slipped, you re-tasted the leeks of Egypt, and now Your soul echoes the cries of bleating sheep that you refused to slaughter.

7. When Samuel faced Saul with his disobedience, Saul responded, "I have sinned." (But I really intended it for good.) He's trying to excuse and cover up his mistake. "I planned to have a big barbecue to honor the Lord."

But Samuel stands his ground: "To obey is better than sacrifice."

<u>Learn the lesson well</u>:

> It is possible to give up wordly amusements, and
> To give God time, talents and tithes.
> You can give goods to feed the poor.
> Even become some kind of missionary.
> You can do all that, and never obey God in giving yourself
> to Him.

**One day when Simon Peter was near the lake, Jesus came by and called him to follow Him. Well, Peter immediately gave up his fishing nets, but it took three years for him to give his total self to the Lord.

In the New Testament, we read, "The Macedonians first gave themselves unto the Lord." And Jesus tells us, "If any man come after me, let him deny himself...." And that means to go and kill those sheep that are a burden to your life and witness, and then to go on to greater victories in the Lord. The Macedonian Christians set the correct pattern in giving Self, then Service, and their Substance. But God is unwilling to be paid off with substance or service, if you do not first give yourself. The trouble with Saul is that he never gave up Saul.

8. The Lord is grieved about Saul and his disobedience so much so that the Bible tells us in 1 Sam.15:35, "The Lord repented that He had made Saul king over Israel."

9. Now let's investigate what is behind all this disobedience? You see, God never asks us to do anything that will hurt us. Samuel puts his words where the real problem is: Read 1 Sam. 15:23a "Rebellion is as the sin of witchcraft, and stubbornness is as iniquity and idolatry."

Of course we are too sophisticated to classify rebellion and stubbornness in the same category as witchcraft and idolatry. We don't, BUT GOD DOES!

Fellows, we can make excuses for ourselves and say that stubborness runs in our mate's family. I want to tell you it affects you and your family as well.

**An older child was told to stay seated in church. He would stand again and look around. His mom grabbed him and told him to sit down, "And stay seated, or else." After a bit, he whispered, I'm sitting down outside, but I'm standing up inside." Stubbornness!

Stubbornness is the root of many wrongs in our lives. It often interferes with our relationship with one another, and if left unresolved, it can interfere in our relationship with the Lord.

You see, stubbornness is a sin, an unslaughtered sheep, that some of God's people hold on to.

**I recall a church member telling me he did not attend prayer meeting at his church. He insinuated he did not need it. I now wonder if this stubbornness caused him to take a gun and kill himself several years later.

There used to be a song that was titled, "I shall not be moved." And that becomes a theme song for Baptists who are backwards about going forward in God's work through the church. "I think we ought to spend that money on missions at home." "We don't need another building."

**A church was in session. They were discussing whether to remodel the sanctuary, or to construct a new one. One portly fellow stood and said, "This sanctuary was good enough for my grandfather, it was good enough for my father, and it is good enough for me. I make the motion that we remodel. And I will give $500.00 to get it done." He sat down heavily. A piece of ceiling tile fell and hit him on the head. He stood immediately and said, "I didn't know this building was in such disrepair. I will give one thousand dollars to remodel it." When he sat down, a near-by saint prayed, "Hit'im again, Lord."

While the Lord is always up ahead urging His church to move forward, some saints dig their heels into the carpet, and adamently declare, "I shall not be moved." And they end up riding a T-model truck all the way to Glory.

Some of these folk have a problem, unslaughtered sheep. Mule stubbornness that refuses to do the right thing.

**In the church I now attend, there is an 82 year-old man. He told me, "I have been in this church a long time. And I have voted against a lot of things they wanted to do. But when the majority votes to do something, I go along with them and help them to get it done." Well amen to that.

I believe God's people need to pay more attention to God's Word before they make final decisions. Psalm 32:8-9 tell us, "I will instruct thee and teach thee in the way thou shalt go... Be ye not as the horse, or the mule, which have no understanding..."

10. The Lord is ever building for eternity. And I don't ever want to build fences where He is trying to build bridges.

11. Now, what should you do with your unslaughtered sheep? Charles Wesley wrote a song "Blessed Be the Name." One of the verses has these words about Christ:

> "He breaks the power of canceled sin,
> He sets the prisoner free,
> His blood can make the foulest clean,
> His blood availed for me."

He is stating through song that Jesus breaks the power of sin that once enslaved you. It is already done when you submit your weakness, your captured sheep to Him. To claim victory over what victimizes you, it takes drastic action on your part.

**To show you what I mean, while Hernando Cortez was conquering Mexico, he and his men sailed up a river to establish a town. When they arrived, Cortez was so committed to this task, he burned the ships they sailed on to keep from being tempted to retreat.

12. The Lord sends Samuel to tell Saul he needed a change of heart to be empowered to do God's thing. Saul had Samuel to goad and guide him. Ahab had his Elijah to reprove and rebuke. David had a Nathan to help him face the truth. Herod had his John the Baptist to shake his conscience.

And I am here to tell you, you will remain a captive to your special sin until, UNTIL you are ready to put it on the sacrificial altar.

Blessed is the man who listens to his prophet, and becomes obedient to the oracles of God. Most of us have had a prophet sometime in our lives, someone who cared, someone willing to risk a relationship, to help a struggling soul to find the right way. This special person could have been a parent, a loving mate, a loyal pastor, an emissary from the Lord. Samuel was that person to Saul, but Saul was unwilling to learn the lesson of obedience, thus God took away his right to be a king. When anybody trifles with God's warning through His agent, the time will come when God ceases to warn - and dismay and disaster ultimately follows.

13. The Lord wants us to bring our brokenness and weaknesses to Him for his healings and restorations. God can use broken things: He uses broken soil to produce our grain. He uses the crushed grain to feed our bodies. The Bible tells us: "A broken and a contrite heart, O Lord, Thou will not despise." God can do nothing with a proud heart. But He can take a heart that is humbled in human weakness and make it into a trophy of His grace. Apart from God we can do nothing of eternal value. With God, we "can do all things through Christ Who strengthens us." Phil. 4:13

14. In the New Testament we find another Saul, he was from Tarsus. Once he was as stubborn and unbroken as Saul the King. But one day God met him on the road to Damascus. He broke Saul down, made him over, and he became the great Apostle Paul.

**In the O.T. Saul started with a crown and ended up with a cross of his own making.

**In the N.T. Saul submitted to a Cross, was "crucified with Christ," and ended with a crown of Glory. Both were headstrong men: One took the road of stubbornness and ended a suicide. The other took the road of submission and became one of the greatest servants of God who ever lived.

Do you get it? God could not then, and He will not now, use unbowed, unbroken, uncrucified people to do His work and will.

—The Gilboa Road, the road King Saul chose, was a sad road.
—The Damascus Road, the road for Saul of Tarsus. is a glad road.

The Gilboa road of stubbornness leads to death, death of conscience, death to the will to follow God. The Damascus road leads to life, an abundant life here. Eternal life hereafter!

<u>CONCLUSION</u>

There are thousands of unslaughtered sheep among God's people. Some hidden, and many unhidden. Bad habits, bad attitudes, misdirected loyalties, and they affect your body, your mind and your relationships. And I want to tell any and all of you who have these problems, God is not pleased with those bleating sheep.

It is up to you to recognize they already interfere with your testimony. They are a heavy burden that causes restlessness in your soul. They build walls between you and fellow Christians.

It is time for you to be honest and say, "It's not my brother, nor my sister, but it's me, O Lord, standing in the need of prayer."

The altar is a place of death. Today is your opportunity to place your unslaughtered, accusing sheep upon the altar. God wants you to do it.

You need to do it.
You know you have planned to do it.
Now is the time.

I want every head bowed and every eye closed. I want to give you this time to put into action the desire of your heart. While the musicians play, I ask you to come up and touch this altar as a sign to God and to yourself, that you are ready to obey God's command and to be set free from any unslaughtered sheep of the past. Now is the time to come. Amen

*"Mary and Martha wanted their brother regenerated,
a good thing. Jesus
gave them a resurrection, a better thing."*

WE MUST LEARN TO WAIT

John 11:1-6; Psalm 27:14.

Lazarus was a friend of Jesus. He had two sisters, Mary and Martha. One day Lazarus became critically ill. The two sisters knew that Jesus loved Lazarus, and they also knew Jesus had the power to heal Lazarus of his illness. So they sent word to Jesus their brother was sick and they needed for the Lord to come to Bethany to heal him.

What did Jesus do? Hurry over there to heal His friend? That seems the logical thing to do. But look in John 11 at verse 6. Jesus waited two days! Now look at verse 17, "He found that (Lazarus) had been in the grave four days." This means between the time the sisters sent for Jesus, more than four days had elapsed. Note what Martha told Jesus in verse 21. "If You had been here, Lazarus would not have died." Meaning: If Jesus had been there to respond to their request, Lazarus would probably still be living.

Was it not normal to ask Jesus to change something those sisters did not want to face? They looked at their brother. He was very ill. They loved him deeply. They knew he might die. They were not ready for that day to arrive.

Now there are some lessons we need to learn in this unfolding story.

I. WE MUST LEARN TO WAIT FOR GOD'S WILL TO BE DONE.

1. This is difficult to do. ** I lost my son, Michael, to a very radical, death-dealing esophageal cancer on January 11, 2006. From the

165

moment the doctor told us Michael had cancer, and showed us the pictures of that horrific, ulcerated sore in his esophagus, I began to pray, and many of my friends joined with me in asking the Lord to heal Michael. After all, he was only 45 years of age. He had a wife, a 24 year-old son, and a 13 year-old daughter. I prayed for him to live because he was my son. I had seen him grow from a tiny baby into childhood. I took him to school. I played with him in the yard. I had dreams for my son. Those dreams did not include illness and death.

Not long after he had finished high school, he married and became the father of a baby boy. And every baby boy has the right to expect his daddy to be there when he has his problems, big and small. He wants his daddy to be best man at his wedding. Heath wanted his daddy to be there and enjoy watching his grandchildren grow and develop. Crystal, Michael's wife, needed him. She has Lupus. Together, she and Michael became parents of a little girl, Miranda. And we prayed, "Please God, let Michael live to see her graduate. And one day to be at her wedding." This seems to have been a reasonable request to the Lord.

2. But the Lord had other plans for Michael. Oh, if we could see Michael today. We would see that he is now fulfilling what the Lord planned for him to be from the day of his conception and birth. God's plan includes eternity for every child of His beyond the grave. If your hope is complete, you must remember our Heavenly Father gives life on both sides of the grave. He gives abundant life here, and eternal life hereafter.

** I really don't know everything that is going on in Heaven. But let me tell you this, there is nothing going on in this earth, nor in your life, that is not going to be 100% better in Glory. "Up There," no time clocks, no bills to pay, no illnesses to create gloom and doom.

** It's even better than Kingfish, who was an actor on the Amos and Andy sitcom, imagined. He said Heaven to him would be "Sitting in a rocking chair, smoking a ten-cent cigar, with a Sears Roebuck catalog in my hands, and having unlimited credit."

3. We simply do not have the vision to see our lives as God sees them. We see our lives unfolding a day at a time, an hour at a time, a second at a time. And because we do not have this long-range vision, where the Lord sees our beginning on earth, while seeing our completion in Heaven, we ask for immediate results. We <u>don't want to wait,</u> not even to wait for a pound cake to rise in the oven.

I remember when we were children. Mama would bake a pound cake. And when Mama baked a pound cake, everybody walked very softly, even talked quietly, as if that cake could hear you and take a sinking nosedive to the middle of the cake pan, if you talked too loud. Then we learned that a pound cake that had fallen seemed to taste better, and crunchier than a fluffy pound cake. Sometimes we would dance around the oven when Mama was out of sight. We didn't care about waiting for that cake to rise.

4. And this is symptomatic of our times. We want to rush, rush to get where we're going, so we can rush someplace else. This rushing all the time unsettles our nerves, eats at our gut, and makes us apprehensive about tomorrow, makes us worry over things that probably won't ever happen. When we worry a lot, we tend to be harsh on people around us. Worry is like rocking in a rocking chair - it will give you something to do, but it won't get you anywhere. It is amazing how some people suffer a lot, and worry so very little, while others worry a lot, and suffer so little. No doubt the great sufferer is cashing in on a sufficient faith and trust in the Lord.

If you are a worrier anyway. let me suggest something positive for you to do. Worry that a man-eating tiger is chasing after you. If you worry about it long enough you'll find that your worrying worked, it kept the tiger away. "That's ridiculous." Of course it is. But let me ask, has any of your worrying ever changed anything?

The reason I point this out, is that we are told in the Bible not to worry. WHY? Because <u>worry is the opposite of trust,</u> and when we trust God to handle our problems and handle our tomorrows, then we can be busy doing something useful, instead of sitting down worrying. Worry is being wasteful of time.

** Medical experts tell us prolonged worry can lead to physical problems: Ulcers, headaches, backaches, high blood pressure, depression, and it even causes heart attacks. Worry will cripple you if you don't control it. It will disrupt spiritual productivity.

Some helpful hints about your worries:

1. Turn worry into prayer. I Peter 5:7"Cast all your care upon Him, for He cares for you."
2. Live one day at a time. Don't allow any tears of yesterday, nor any fears of tomorrow, to dominate your today.
3. Don't worry about anything that is out of your control. Duh?

Listen, the Lord has engineered you so that you reflect what you're thinking. You act out every thought with your body language, or your smile or non-smile. Proverbs 23:7, "As a man thinketh within himself, so he is." Whatever you allow yourself to think that is the way you feel and appear to people who see you.

** When I was in my pre-teens, I went to see the movie, "Frankenstein." And when that monster came walking into the picture, I closed my eyes. Terrified! And many youngsters around me screamed in horror. Now, let me tell you his, that moving picture scared me that day, and it scared me for days, months, even years. Yes, I knew the monster was Boris Karloff. I knew the movie was make-believe. But I allowed that movie to imprint my soul. And I wasted many an hour worrying that monster would come out from under my bed, or come from behind a tree, and he might gobble me up. It took a lot of running and growing for me to come to a place where I did what every thinking person must do to find peace, contentment and serenity in my life. Do you know how I became a victor over my ghosts and nightmares? It took a long time. But one day I came face to face with my past that condemned my future. I came to a dead-end in my life. All I saw ahead of me was wastefulness, emptiness, loneliness, hopelessness. I thought I had no options. I felt somewhat like Martha and Mary. "Our brother is dead. We can do nothing about it. All we can do is accept the inevitable. Death. Loss and constant misery."

This leads to the second point in this message:
So, number one - We must learn to wait for God's will to be done.

II. WE MUST BELIEVE GOD HAS PURPOSE IN OUR WAITING

While we wait, we might have to suffer. But suffering produces patience. Romans 5:3, "Tribulation worketh patience." The Living Bible puts it this way: "Problems, they help us to learn to be patient." Thus, suffering can create qualities of Godly character within us. When we are willing to wait. Waiting implies expectation. Look at an amaryllis bulb. It appears to look so dirty and unpromising. Yet, when you put it in dirt, fertilize and water it, and place it in the sun, one day, according to God's calendar, it bursts forth into beautiful shades of brilliant color. (Many of our problems are intensified because we want God's resources, but we are unwilling to wait for God's schedule.) And what we wait for may not be as important as what happens to us while we wait.

1. When we have come to the end of our own rope, we must believe we are at the beginning of God's rope of repair and renewal. So, what do you do when you have tried every way you can to restructure your life - and it still remains fractured and broken? There seems to be no light at the end of the tunnel.

2. We must believe in, and we must rely on, Someone to fix it for us. What would you do if you had a broken leg? Why you would go to an orthopedic doctor. What would you do if your heart begins to fail? You'd go to a cardiologist. What would you do if your house caught on fire? Call the fire department. Then what would you do when your life is all twisted up, and you try everything you know to fix it? Yet, nothing you do is sufficient. You make resolutions,

and then break them before a week is over. What can you do? What must you do? You must do what I did, I called upon the One who made me and gave me a soul like unto His Spirit. I had to put myself into His hands to fix me, and into His care for keeping me.

Remember what happened when Martha and Mary asked Jesus to come and heal their brother? "Heal him now." I stood by Michael's bedside, and I wanted him to live one more day. And if God had allowed one day, I would have asked for another, and another, and another. That's what those sisters wanted from Jesus.

 But Jesus had something better. The sisters wanted a regeneration, a good thing; but Jesus gave them a resurrection, a better thing! Can you imagine the thrill of that moment when Jesus went to the tomb of Lazarus. And anybody who saw Him would be thinking. "He loved Lazarus, and He is going to the tomb to weep for him." Instead of weeping, He spoke to that dead body and showed the whole world He has control over deadness, **"Lazarus, come forth."** And when Jesus said that, the bones of Lazarus began to quiver. His heart began to beat, his blood began to flow through his body, his brain began to function, he opened his eyes, he got up and he walked out of that tomb of death. LISTEN! You can't be around Jesus and stay dead!

3. Where is your faith today? Is it burdened down with doubt?

> Are you at a standstill in time?
> Are you sinking in a quagmire of uncertainty?

Listen to this promise from God to you: "Wait on the Lord." That means you must be willing to wait for His timing. Wait for His unfolding will in your life. "The wheels of God grind slowly, but they grind exceedingly small." In your impatience, and in your night of suffering, you must have faith to believe God is ready to give you His Sonrise. Don't try to run ahead of Him. If you do, you'll mess up His program that He has for you.

** To run ahead of the Lord is like the little boy who was out in his backyard. He came into the house, and his mother asked, "What have you been doing out in the yard?" "Helping God." "How have you been helping God?" "I been helping Him to open rosebuds." Well! Take it from me, an old rose bud opener. When you interfere with God's timing. When you try to rush tomorrow, when you try to outguess what the Lord is going to do for you. You mess with God's schedule and try to change things that you think need to be changed; or you want to stand still when God says it's time to move on. You do that and your days will be filled with more frustration than faith can overcome. Do that, and you will miss God's boat every time. Listen! "Be still." Wait! "For I am God."

III. A FINAL WORD: GOD'S BEST IS ALWAYS AHEAD FOR YOU WHO WALK WITH TRUSTING FAITH IN HIS ONLY BEGOTTEN SON.

Isaiah 40: 31, "They that wait upon the Lord shall renew their strength."

1. This is the kind of waiting that gives you rest and readies you for further adventures with the Lord.

This is my second book. A book of sermons. The gracious Lord has given me another sweet Christian wife to walk with me, to comfort and to encourage me. And now, every day is sweeter than the day before. I'm marching to Zion.

I have my sights set on Heavenly things. I waited. I waited on the Lord, and He has strengthened my heart. "Wait," God says, "Wait on the Lord."

Amen!

Printed in the United States
50760LVS00004B/175-204